THE
GREAT
GIFT
BOOK

THE GREAT GIFT BOOK

WENDY EVERETT

Photography by Kit DeFever

CHILTON BOOK COMPANY
Radnor, Pennsylvania

Copyright © 1986 by Wendy Everett
All Rights Reserved
Published in Radnor, Pennsylvania 19089 by Chilton Book Company

Designed by Adrianne Onderdonk Dudden
Manufactured in the United States of America

Library of Congress Cataloging in Publication Data
Everett, Wendy.
   The great gift book.
   Includes index.
   1. Needlework—Patterns.   2. House furnishings.
3. Gifts.   I. Title.
TT753.E93   1986   746.4   86-47613
ISBN 0-8019-7742-8 (hardcover)
ISBN 0-8019-7716-9 (pbk.)

1 2 3 4 5 6 7 8 9 0   5 4 3 2 1 0 9 8 7 6

A special thanks to the following people without whom I could not have written this book!

Mom, Dad, Grandma Everett, Susan, Dennis, Sarah, John, Karen, Jessica, Carol, Dave, Kit de Fever, Julie Wyckoff, Patricia Sorin, Anne Hall, Karen Seltzer, Jason Sapan, and Dianne, Danny and Jesse Minc.

COVER: *Grapevine Wreath with Hearts, Signature Pillow, Lace Teddy Bear Sachet, Cross Stitch "I Love You," Embroidered Heart Box, Friendship Pillow, Signature Quilt. All in Chapter 1.*

CONTENTS

THE
GREAT
GIFT
BOOK

INTRODUCTION

« The Art of Gift Giving »

There is more to giving a gift than buying something, wrapping it, and handing it to someone. That is why people make gifts. A handmade gift is a gift from the heart becasue it is a labor of love, representing time, energy, and caring. A handmade gift bears the personal touch of the one who created it and is cherished by the one who receives it for that reason. That is why the handmade gift of today often becomes the treasured family heirloom of tomorrow.

But there is more to gift giving, even handmade gift giving. There is the *art* of gift giving. This is the art of making your handmade gift especially personal and the art of presenting your gift in an unusual or unexpected way. The only requirements for practicing this art are a little imagination and thoughtfulness. For example, if you are going to give a little niece a Tooth Fairy pillow, why not also include a letter from the Tooth Fairy herself, written on paper in the shape of a tooth? I'm sure this will bring an especially big smile to her face! Or if your daughter has just had her first baby and you want to give her a handmade lace baby quilt, why not make it extra special by embroidering the lullabye you used to sing her to sleep with on the quilt back? You'll be creating a gift that is sure to stay in the family for generations.

This book provides you with a beautiful assortment of gift ideas for every occasion—gifts for friends, family, brides, babies, and children—everything from what to give your best friend when she moves away to what to give to your grandson to help teach him his ABCs. Better yet, this book provides you with creative and fun suggestions for giving your gift in a special way. Just look for the gift-giving ideas following the instructions for each project. Before you know it you'll be practicing the art of gift giving—and loving it too!

« General Construction Notes »

1. All seams are $\frac{1}{4}''$ unless otherwise specified.

2. It is always advisable to wash fabric to pre-shrink it before sewing. This is especially advisable when making a quilt, since several types of fabric are used together and one may shrink more than another, causing puckering.

3. If organza ribbon is difficult to find, you can make your own by cutting strips of the specified dimensions from organza fabric. Cut on the bias so that the edges don't unravel.

4. When stuffing lace with potpourri, always line the lace with organza first. Also be sure to use a small stitch setting, 15-20 stitches per inch, so that the lace will not unravel when the seam is trimmed and turned.

5. In cases where the potpourri doesn't show, such as in felt sachets, poly stuffing can be used for the stuffing and a concentrated liquid sachet can be used to scent them. Put several drops on a cotton ball and place it in the middle of the stuffing.

6. If your potpourri sachets begin to lose some of their scent after a while, revive them by spraying with a canned scent, favorite perfume spray, or by adding a few drops of concentrated liquid scent in an inconspicuous spot such as on the ribbon roses.

7. The easiest way to transfer a design is to slip the pattern under the fabric and trace the design with a disappearing ink pen or a water-soluble pen. Use the disappearing ink pen when you will be able to complete the embroidery within 24 hours. Use the water-soluble pen when your embroidery will be more time-consuming. Holding the fabric and pattern up to a sunny window will help you see the lines more clearly. You can also make a "light box" for yourself by placing a piece of glass over a lampshade with a wide opening at the top. Use a high wattage light bulb. If neither of these methods work, you can transfer your design using dressmaker's carbon and a tracing wheel. There are also a variety of transfer pens on the market that can be purchased in a craft or fabric shop.

8. When embellishing a pillow or quilt with lace ruffle, always do these two things. If the project has corners, gather or fold over $\frac{1}{2}''$ to $1\frac{1}{2}''$ of ruffle at each corner. This will allow the ruffle to stay flat when the project is completed. Also, be sure to check your seams for any bit of "stray" ruffle that may be caught in them before you trim. This means turning your project right side out to check, and then turning it back to trim. It's a little extra work, but well worth it!

GIFTS FOR FRIENDS
AND FAMILY

« Grapevine Wreath with Hearts »

16" diameter grapevine wreath
⅛ yd 36"-wide orange gingham
⅛ yd 36"-wide rust calico fabric
1 bunch each: baby's breath, yellow
   straw flowers, orange straw flowers
Brown floral tape
Scallop or pinking shears
Polyester stuffing
4 yd ⅞"-wide brown/rust/orange
   patchwork craft ribbon

Craft glue
Brown or black heavy-duty thread
Large-eye needle
2 yd ½"-wide beige ruffled lace
1 18" length 30-gauge cotton-covered
   wrapping wire
1½ 9" × 12" squares gold felt

1. Use 5 ft of the patchwork ribbon to make the loops of the bow. To do this, fold the ribbon over itself so that there are approximately 5 loops on each end. Gather the center of the loops with a tight twist of a 9" length of wire. Open the loops.

2. Use a 1 ft length to form the streamers on the bow. To do this, fold the ribbon in half, gather 1" from the fold, and twist with a 9" length of wire. Pull the streamers down to one side and cut the ends in a V shape. Puff the "knot" and place this knot-and-streamer section into the center of the loops and secure with the wire ends. (See Perfect Bows, page 115.) Attach the bow to the wreath either at the top of the wreath, as shown in Fig. 1-1, or off to one side, as indicated in Fig. 1-4. Wrap the remaining ribbon around the wreath, securing the ends with glue.

3. With scallop or pinking shears, cut 6 hearts from gold felt using Fig. 1-2 as a pattern. Using matching thread, stitch 2 hearts together, stitching ¼"

Fig. 1-1 Grapevine wreath with hearts.

in from edge and leaving open between dots. Stuff and stitch closed. Make 3 gold hearts.

    4. Cut 6 hearts from calico and 6 hearts from gingham, using Fig. 1-3 as a pattern. With right sides and raw edges together, baste the lace trim to 3 calico and 3 gingham hearts. Right sides together, pin the matching hearts to the lace-trimmed ones, and stitch ¼″ from the edge, leaving open between dots. Trim seams, clip curves, turn right side out, press, stuff, and slip stitch closed. Make 3 calico and 3 gingham hearts.

    5. Cut 9 18″ lengths of heavy-duty thread. Sew a length through the back of each heart and tie the hearts onto the wreath as shown in Fig. 1-4.

    6. Make 17 bunches of assorted dried flowers, wrapping the ends with brown floral tape. Dip the ends in glue and push into the wreath to make a pleasing arrangement.

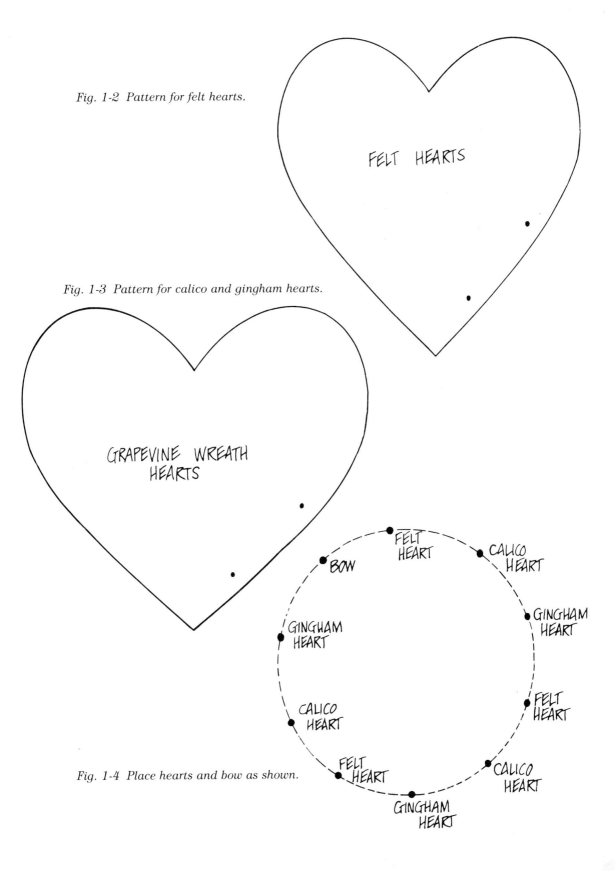

Fig. 1-2 Pattern for felt hearts.

FELT HEARTS

Fig. 1-3 Pattern for calico and gingham hearts.

GRAPEVINE WREATH
HEARTS

Fig. 1-4 Place hearts and bow as shown.

BOW
FELT HEART
CALICO HEART
GINGHAM HEART
FELT HEART
CALICO HEART
GINGHAM HEART
FELT HEART
CALICO HEART
GINGHAM HEART

Special Ideas for Giving

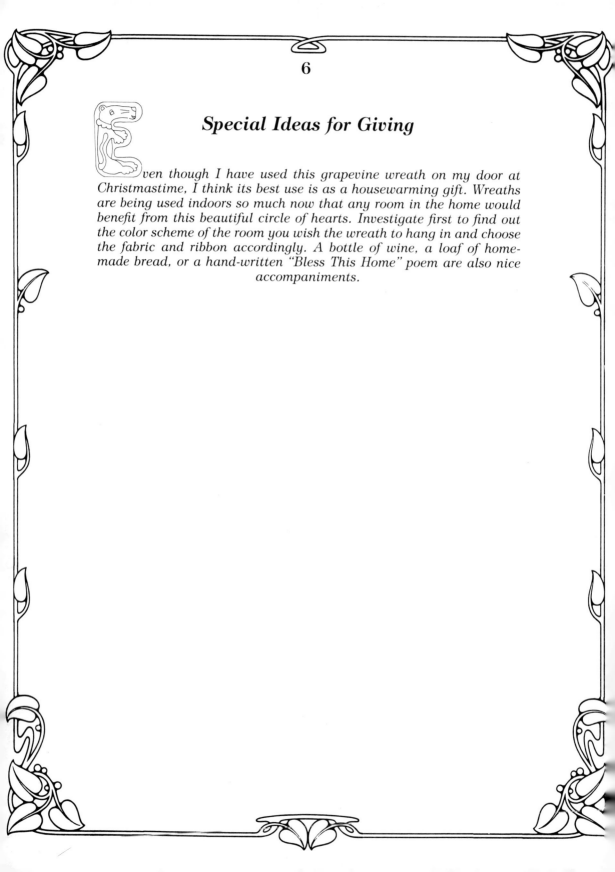

Even though I have used this grapevine wreath on my door at Christmastime, I think its best use is as a housewarming gift. Wreaths are being used indoors so much now that any room in the home would benefit from this beautiful circle of hearts. Investigate first to find out the color scheme of the room you wish the wreath to hang in and choose the fabric and ribbon accordingly. A bottle of wine, a loaf of home-made bread, or a hand-written "Bless This Home" poem are also nice accompaniments.

« Friendship Pillow »

10" square ecru Aida cloth (11 squares
  per inch)
10" square print fabric
Poly stuffing
6"-diameter embroidery hoop

Embroidery floss: pink, yellow, light
  blue, light green, dark blue, and
  brown
Blunt-tipped embroidery needle
1 yd 1"-wide ecru eyelet ruffle

1. Place the Aida cloth square into the embroidery hoop. Find the center of the cloth and embroider the design, following the chart (Fig. 1-6). Remove the embroidery hoop and press the embroidered piece, using a pressing cloth.

2. Cut the Aida cloth into a 10"-diameter circle. Pin the eyelet ruffle to the Aida cloth, right sides together and raw edges even, with the ruffle ends at the bottom of the pillow. Stitch the ruffle ends together, right sides together. Press. Topstitch the seam. Baste the ruffle to the Aida cloth.

3. Cut a 10" circle from the print fabric. Pin this to the Aida cloth right sides together. Stitch, leaving open 3" at the bottom. Trim the seam, turn right side out and press. Stuff the pillow and slip stitch the opening closed.

Fig. 1-5 Friendship pillow.

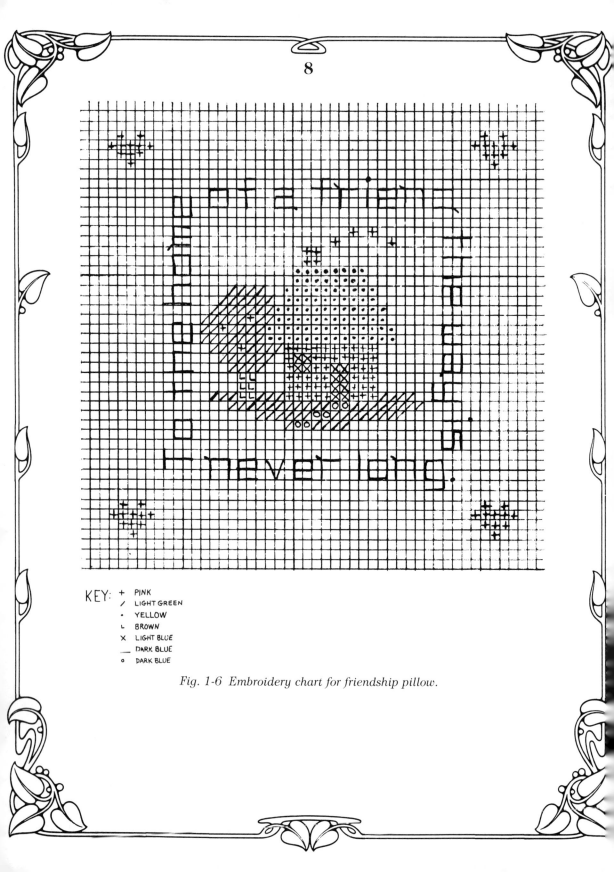

KEY: + PINK
/ LIGHT GREEN
• YELLOW
L BROWN
X LIGHT BLUE
— DARK BLUE
o DARK BLUE

Fig. 1-6 Embroidery chart for friendship pillow.

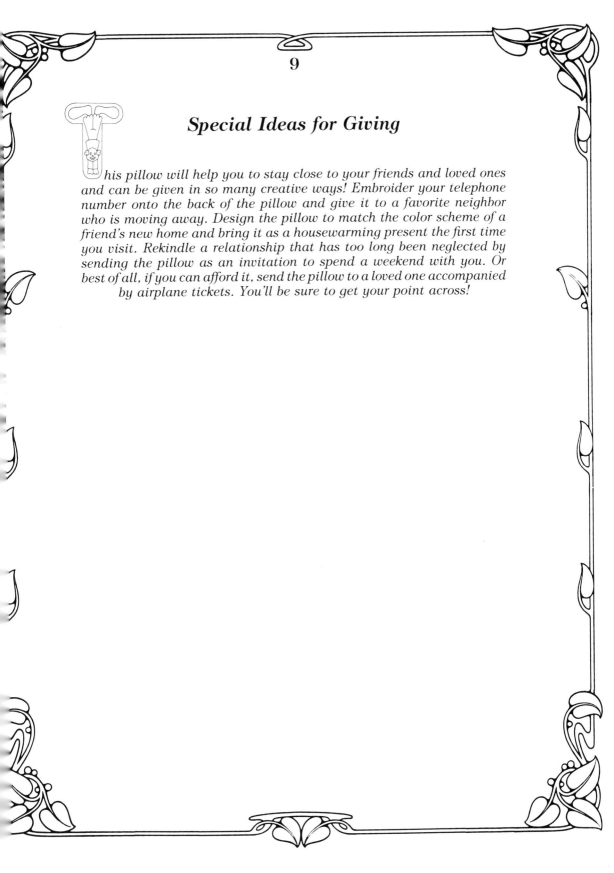

Special Ideas for Giving

his pillow will help you to stay close to your friends and loved ones and can be given in so many creative ways! Embroider your telephone number onto the back of the pillow and give it to a favorite neighbor who is moving away. Design the pillow to match the color scheme of a friend's new home and bring it as a housewarming present the first time you visit. Rekindle a relationship that has too long been neglected by sending the pillow as an invitation to spend a weekend with you. Or best of all, if you can afford it, send the pillow to a loved one accompanied by airplane tickets. You'll be sure to get your point across!

« Embroidered Heart Box »

½ yd. 45″-wide muslin
Candlewicking thread
Pink embroidery thread
Embroidery needle
4″ diameter embroidery hoop

2 ft ⅜″-wide pink satin ribbon
2 ft ¾″-wide beige lace ruffle
Disappearing ink pen
½ yd 45″-wide poly batting

1. To make a heart pattern, fold an 8½-×-11-inch piece of paper in half, unfold it, place the fold along the dashed line in Fig. 1-8, and trace the half heart onto the paper. Refold and cut out the heart. With the disappearing ink pen, trace the heart outline onto a piece of muslin. Transfer the embroidery design to the center of this muslin heart, as shown in Fig. 1-9.

2. Place the muslin in the hoop and embroider using these stitches:
a. Using 2 strands of candlewicking, work the lattice center using a long stitch.

Fig. 1-7 Embroidered heart box.

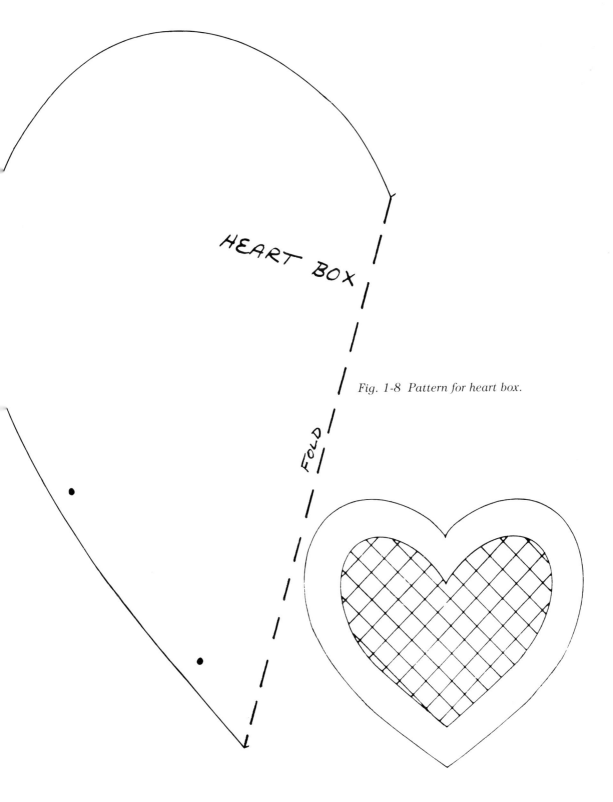

HEART BOX

FOLD

Fig. 1-8 Pattern for heart box.

Fig. 1-9 Embroidery design for heart box.

    b. Using 2 strands of pink floss, embroider a small "plus" sign where each of the candlewick threads cross.

    c. Using 2 strands of candlewicking thread, work French knots around the edges of the lattice work.

    d. Using 2 strands of candlewicking thread, embroider a chain stitch around the larger heart outline.

    3. Cut out the embroidered heart. With right sides together, sew on the lace ruffle close to the edge.

    4. Cut out a second muslin heart and place it over the first, right sides together. Cut out 2 batting hearts and place them under the embroidered heart. Pin together and stitch using a ¼″ seam, leaving open between the dots. Trim the seam, clip the curves, turn and press. Slip stitch the opening closed.

    5. Make a second padded heart just as the first without the embroidery and ruffle. This will be the bottom of the box.

    6. Cut out 2 rectangles of muslin 4″ × 23″ long. Cut out 2 pieces of batting the same size. Place the 2 pieces of muslin on top of the 2 pieces of batting and pin. Stitch using a ¼″ seam, leaving open on one end. Trim the seam turn and press. Slip stitch the open end closed. Topstitch through all thicknesses 1″ in from each long edge.

    7. Fold this rectangle in half lengthwise and press. Hand topstitch at the fold through all thicknesses to strengthen the point of the heart.

    8. Stitch the ends of the rectangle together ½″ in from the edges. Sew this piece by hand to the bottom of the box.

    9. Place the top heart on the box and sew on by hand at the two uppermost curves of the heart. Make two ribbon bows and sew over these two points.

Special Ideas for Giving

Such a beautiful box should never go empty! Fill it with something that's sure to please, like the recipient's favorite homemade cookies, wrapped carefully in colorful tissue paper. Or make a batch of heart-shaped sugar cookies, frost with pink icing, and decorate with a candy heart printed with a love message. This way the lucky person can "read between the bites"! Include the recipe if you wish.

« Signature Quilt »

This quilt (Fig. 1-17) was made for my grandmother's 90th birthday celebration. Each member of the family was asked to submit an embroidered signature on a 9" square of fabric, choosing the floss and fabric colors they most preferred. The back of the quilt was embroidered with a very large "We love you Grandma!" and her birthday date. Some of these squares came from as far away as Australia! Children too young to have a signature had their names embroidered in block letters. Small identifying marks such as hearts, flowers, or nicknames were also addded. Needless to say Grandma loved it!

Finished dimensions of the quilt are $42\frac{1}{2}''$ by 51".

30 9" squares assorted color fabric
$1\frac{1}{2}$ yd 45"-wide fabric for the backing
(color of your choice)
Quilt batting
Assorted colors embroidery floss
7"-diameter embroidery hoop

Embroidery needle
Disappearing ink pen
Black fine-tipped marker
9" squares white paper
#8 DMC embroidery thread to
coordinate with backing

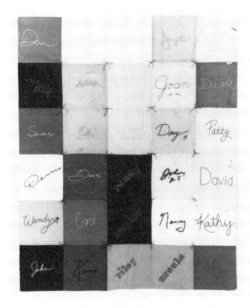

Fig. 1-17 Signature quilt.

1. Have each person sign his or her name in the middle of a 9″ square of paper with the black marker, being sure to leave at least a 1″ border. Ask each person what their favorite two colors are and note on the paper. Transfer each signature to a 9″ square of fabric by placing the paper beneath the fabric and tracing with the disappearing ink pen. Choose fabric and floss according to the person's favorite colors. Embroider the names using a stem or back stitch. (Note: You may want to make a rough layout of the squares before beginning to get an idea of the coloration of the finished quilt. Different shades of the same color can be used for variation, or the names can be placed in a different order to achieve a pleasing color result.)

2. Sew the squares together following your layout. Use a ¼″ seam. Sew the squares into rows and then sew the rows together, matching the corners and pressing the seams. Set aside.

3. Cut the quilt backing fabric to match the dimensions of the quilt top. Write an appropriate message on the back in disappearing ink and embroider it using the #8 DMC embroidery thread. You can write the message freehand or use the block letter alphabet in Chapter 6.

4. Cut the quilt batting to size, ironing out any folds. Place it on a clean surface. Place the quilt top over the quilt batting, right side up. Place the quilt backing over this, right side down. Pin together and stitch around all edges, using a ¼″ seam and leaving a one foot opening in the center of the bottom edge. Turn, press and slip stitch the opening closed.

5. Use the remaining #8 DMC embroidery thread to tack the quilt together at the corners of each square. Cut 1 ft lengths of thread to do this, and tie in bows to finish.

Special Ideas for Giving

his is the kind of important gift that begs for a very special occasion such as a 50th wedding anniversary or a 90th birthday. Make the quilt even more personal by embroidering a special message on the back. This message can be as simple as "I Love You" surrounded by Xs and Os for kisses and hugs, or it could be a favorite verse from a song, poem, or the Bible. Of course, everyone who has had a hand in its creation will want to be present at the unwrapping, so plan a party and be sure to include someone who has a video camera. You're going to want to remember this day!

Gifts for children: *Ballerina Puppet, Bunny Puppet, Heart Mobile, Circus ABC Counted Cross Stitch Name, Felt Animal Sachets, Tooth Fairy Pillow, Circus Alphabet Quilt.*

Gifts for baby: *Teddy Bear Birth Announcement, Bib with Bunny Toy, Heart Doll, Crib Hearts, Lace Baby Quilt and Pillow, Baby Bib with Chicken Scratch Heart, Baby Jars with Chicken Scratch Heart Lids.*

Gifts for a wedding: *Potpourri Lace Hoop, Heart Picture Frame, Scented Padded Hanger, Hanging Heart Sachet, Potpourri Travel Roll-up Bag, Mini Sachets, Lace Potpourri Pillow, Ring Bearer Pillow.*

Circus Alphabet Quilt.

« Signature Pillow »

Courtesy of Jane Nickel

½ yd 36"-wide muslin
15" square ¼"-thick batting
2 yd 2½"-wide muslin ruffle
2 yd 1¼"-wide beige lace ruffle
Embroidery floss: light blue and dark
  blue

Embroidery needle
Small embroidery hoop
Poly stuffing
Fabric marking pen with water-soluble
  ink

1. Measure a 15½" square on the muslin fabric and cut it out.

2. Measure a 17½" square, centering it on the remaining muslin. Do not cut out. Divide this square into 25 3½" squares. Do not cut apart. Ask the people involved in the signature pillow to sign their names in the center of these squares, using the pen with water-soluble ink. Embroider the names

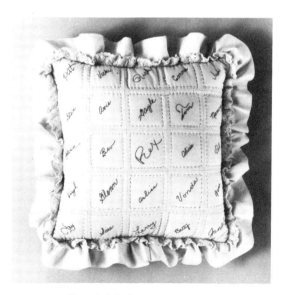

Fig. 1-18 Signature pillow.

using a stem stitch with three strands of dark blue floss. When all the embroidery is completed, rinse to remove the ink, press and cut out the squares.

3. Sew the squares together in the proper order using $\frac{1}{4}''$ seams. Sew the squares into rows first and then sew the rows together. Press the seams.

4. Pin the stitched squares to the batting and quilt $\frac{1}{4}''$ from the seams using the light blue floss. (Along the outside edges you will be quilting $\frac{1}{2}''$ from the edges.)

5. Sew the lace ruffle to the muslin ruffle. Pin this ruffle to the quilted piece of muslin, raw edges together, starting and ending at the bottom left corner. Stitch the ruffle to itself at this corner on a 45-degree slant and cut off the excess. Press the seam and topstitch. Baste around all edges.

6. Embroider a message onto the $15\frac{1}{2}''$ square of muslin if desired. Pin this piece to the pillow front right sides together. Stitch $\frac{1}{4}''$ from edges, leaving open 6″ at the bottom edge. Trim the seam, turn and press. Stuff and slip stitch the opening closed.

Special Ideas for Giving

he signature pillow is a perfect gift for a fellow worker at retirement. Instead of everyone chipping in money for a store-bought gift that anyone could have, everyone is giving a little piece of themselves to make a gift that the retiree will cherish forever. To make this gift extra special, with your co-workers select a saying to be embroidered on the pillow back. Is there some phrase the retiring friend is always saying at work? Have fellow workers given the retiree a nickname? Choose some idiosyncrasy and capitalize upon it. Then enjoy watching as your friend opens up this special gift at the retirement party!

GIFTS FOR A WEDDING

« Ring Bearer Pillow »

10" × 20" piece white satin fabric
5½ ft white lace ruffle, 6" wide
Disappearing ink pen
Poly stuffing
Potpourri or concentrated liquid sachet
1 yd ¼"-wide white satin ribbon

Glue
White thread
Needle
⅝"-wide doubleface satin ribbon: 4 ft
  each pink, yellow, lilac, and blue
4" ¼"-wide white elastic

Fig. 2-1 Ring bearer pillow.

1. To make the pillow pattern, fold a large piece of paper in half, unfold it, place the fold along the dashed line in Fig. 2-2, and trace Fig. 2-2. Refold and trace the remaining half. Using the pillow pattern, cut out two circles of white satin fabric.

2. Fold the white lace ruffle in half, wrong sides together. Pin this double ruffle to one of the satin circles, right sides and raw edges together, leaving a 1″ excess on each end of the ruffle. Now cut the fold. Pin the ends of one ruffle together, right sides together and stitch, starting with a 1″ seam where the ruffle is pinned to the pillow and tapering to a ¼″ seam at the ruffle edge. This will give the ruffle the extra fullness needed to fall nicely. Trim the seam to ¼″ and press. Finish the other ruffle ends in the same way. Both seams will be "hidden" between the ruffles.

3. Baste the ruffle to the satin circle. Pin the other satin circle over the ruffled one, right sides together. Stitch, leaving open between the dots and being careful not to catch any of the free lace ruffle in the seam. Trim and turn right side out. Press.

4. Cut 6 8″ lengths of each color of ribbon. Following the instructions for the folded ribbon rose in Chapter 5, make six roses of each color ribbon. (Note: Instead of securing the rose with a wrap of wire, secure with a few stitches of white thread, passing the needle through the center of the rose and back to the base to make sure the rose won't pop open.)

5. With the seamed ruffle ends at the bottom of the pillow, trace the heart shape onto the right side of the pillow with the disappearing ink pen. Place the roses along this line, pinning as you place and alternating the colors so that all the roses fit on. Unpin the roses one by one and glue to the satin. (Make sure the glue does not pass through the satin to the back of the pillow.)

6. Stuff the pillow with poly stuffing and potpourri (or insert a cotton ball with a few drops of liquid sachet scent on it). Slip stitch the opening closed.

7. Cut the yard of ¼″ white satin ribbon in half and knot the ends. Sew the center of these pieces of ribbon to the Xs shown on the pattern. Tie in bows.

8. Turning under ¼″ on each end of the elastic, sew by hand to the underside of the pillow, in the center of the pillow. This will serve as a hand hold for the ring bearer.

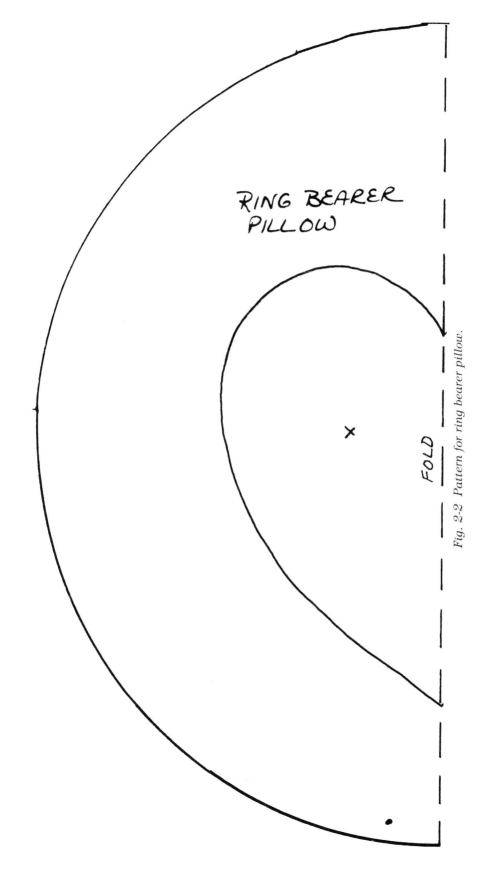

RING BEARER
PILLOW

×

FOLD

Fig. 2-2 Pattern for ring bearer pillow.

Special Ideas For Giving

This pillow is especially beautiful when made to match the bride's dress and the wedding party's colors. If the bride's dress is being hand-made, see if you can obtain some of the fabric and lace to make the pillow, choosing a lace ruffle to coordinate. For the roses, choose satin ribbon that matches the bridesmaids' dresses as closely as possible. Another nice touch is to embroider the names of the wedding party onto the back of the pillow along with the date of the wedding. Now you have created a beautiful showpiece for the ring bearer to hold and also a lovely memento for the bride to cherish.

« Hanging Heart Sachet »

18″ × 10″ peach silk
4 15″ lengths beige organza ribbon, 1⅜″
  wide (or organza fabric cut on the
  bias)
1 ft off-white ½″-wide satin picot-edge
  ribbon

Glue
Poly batting
Potpourri or concentrated liquid scent
1 yd 6″-wide off-white lace ruffle
1 yd 30-gauge wrapping wire

1. Trace Fig. 2-4 onto a folded piece of paper to make a heart pattern. Cut out two silk hearts. Fold the lace ruffle in half right sides together and stitch the ends together. Trim and press the seam. Turn the ruffle right side out.

2. Position the seam so that it will hang in the back of the heart at the bottom point and pin the lace ruffle to the right side of one fabric heart, raw edges together, centering the ruffle. Baste.

3. Pin the ends of the picot-edge ribbon to the heart at the squares shown on the pattern and stitch several times to secure.

4. Pin the other fabric heart over the first one, being careful not to catch

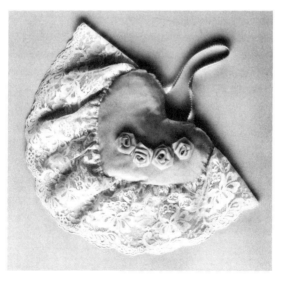

Fig. 2-3 Hanging heart sachet.

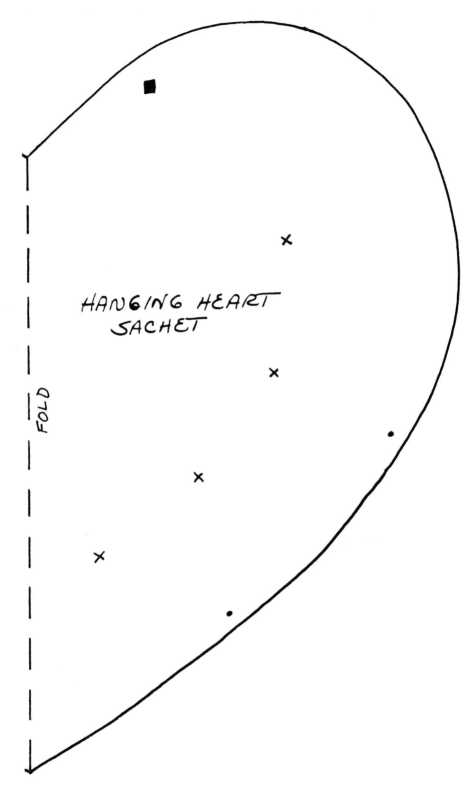

HANGING HEART
SACHET

FOLD

Fig. 2-4 Pattern for hanging heart sachet.

any lace or ribbon in the seam. Stitch around the heart leaving open between the dots. Trim the seam, turn and press.

5. Stuff with poly stuffing, including either some potpourri or concentrated scent. Slip stitch the opening closed. Make four ribbon roses according to the instructions in Chapter 5 and glue to the heart at the Xs.

Special Ideas For Giving

his is the perfect gift when a special occasion calls for dresses to be handmade, such as a wedding. Save a piece of fabric from each of the bridesmaids' dresses and use it to make the heart, color coordinating the ribbon roses and lace. The bride can give these heart sachets to her bridesmaids as a thankful memento of the special day, perhaps tucking in a gift of jewelry, such as pierced earrings which can be attached like dewdrops to the roses. By the same token, the mother of the bride or the maid of honor can make a heart sachet with an extra bit of satin and lace from the bride's dress. When the wedding dress is safely tucked away, this heart sachet will be there to keep the memories of the day alive!

« Lace Potpourri Pillow »

2 12"-×-10" rectangles off-white lace
2 12"-×-10" rectangles white satin
1 yd ½"-wide pink satin picot-edge
  ribbon
1 yd ½"-wide white satin picot-edge
  ribbon

Potpourri (rosebuds if possible)
Poly stuffing
1½ yd 6"-wide off-white lace ruffle
1½ yd 7"-wide off-white lace ruffle (of a
  different style)

1. Baste one lace rectangle to the right side of one satin rectangle. Baste the other lace rectangle to the other satin rectangle, leaving a 4" opening. Place the potpourri rosebuds carefully between these two layers of fabric, arranging them as desired. Baste the opening closed.

2. Starting at the lower left corner, pin the 6"-wide ruffle to the right side of the potpourri-stuffed lace rectangle, raw edges together, making a pleat of 1½" extra lace at each corner and leaving 1" extra on the lower left corner where the lace ruffle begins and ends. Stitch these raw ends right sides together and trim the seam. Baste the ruffle to the rectangle. Do the same with the 7" ruffle.

Fig. 2-5 Lace potpourri pillow.

3. Pin the second lace rectangle over the first, right sides together, being careful not to catch any of the lace ruffle in the seam. Stitch around the raw edges, leaving a 4″ opening. Trim the seam and turn right side out. Press carefully.

4. Stuff the pillow with poly stuffing, putting in some potpourri or liquid sachet scent if desired. Slip stitch the opening closed.

5. Tie the two satin picot-edge ribbons together in a bow and sew near one corner of the pillow. Tie knots in the ribbon ends.

Special Ideas For Giving

ave you ever seen a prettier way to preserve flowers from the bride's bouquet? Dry them following the instructions in Chapter 5 and sprinkle them between the layers of lace and satin. If the bride has earmarked her bouquet for tossing, use flowers from one of the wedding arrangements. Or perhaps each of the bridesmaids will donate a rosebud to the cause. Choosing fabric, lace, and ribbon to match or coordinate with the wedding party's outfits will make the pillow even more cherishable.

« Potpourri Lace Hoop »

10" diameter wooden hoop
12" to 13"-diameter lace doily
Potpourri
1 ft $\frac{1}{2}$"-wide off-white satin picot-edge
  ribbon

1 yd 2"-wide off-white lace ruffle
Craft glue
12"-diameter white organza circle
12"-diameter muslin circle
Poly stuffing

1. Place the doily over the organza and insert into the hoop, stretching slightly so that the doily is flat.

2. Turn the hoop over and sprinkle with potpourri so that the organza is completely covered. Fill in the rest of the space with poly stuffing. (This will save you from using too much potpourri and also keep the potpourri from shifting to the bottom when the hoop is hung.) Put in enough stuffing to secure the potpourri.

3. Spread glue onto the backedge of the wooden hoop and place the muslin circle over this. Press the muslin to the hoop until the glue is dry. Carefully trim off the excess muslin and organza.

Fig. 2-6 Potpourri lace hoop.

4. Spread a second layer of glue along the back edge of the hoop over the muslin. Starting at the top of the hoop, pin the lace ruffle to the hoop, turning under $\frac{1}{2}''$ at the ends. To pin, push the pins on an angle between the two wooden sections of the hoop approximately $\frac{1}{4}''$ apart.

5. Tie the ribbon into a bow and glue over the screw at the top of the hoop.

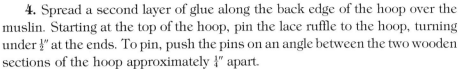

Special Ideas For Giving

he potpourri lace hoop is a lovely way to preserve those wedding day memories! Use a piece of lace left over from making the wedding dress, or use an heirloom crocheted doily, and fill with a potpourri made of flowers from the wedding. With a little planning, this gift could become an expression of the classic wedding saying: "Something old, something new, something borrowed, something blue." Use Grandma's old lace doily, a bit of new lace ruffle, perhaps one that matches the lace of the wedding dress, a potpourri made of flowers borrowed from the wedding, and top it off with a blue satin bow!

« Mini Sachets »

MINI PILLOW SACHET

2 5" squares pink satin
Poly stuffing
Potpourri or concentrated liquid scent

2 ft 2½"-wide lace ruffle
18" length ¼"-wide pink satin picot-edge
  ribbon

1. Starting at the lower left corner, pin the lace ruffle to one of the satin squares, having right sides and raw edges together. Gather about 1" extra of ruffle at each corner so that the ruffle will lie flat when the pillow is finished. Stitch the ruffle ends together and press.

2. Baste the ruffle to the satin square. Pin the other satin square over this first one, right sides together. Stitch around the edges, being careful not to catch any lace in the seam. Leave a 2" opening on one side.

3. Trim, turn and press. Stuff the pillow with poly stuffing and add either potpourri or concentrated liquid sachet. Slip stitch the opening closed.

4. Tie the ribbon in a bow, knot the ends, and sew near one corner of the pillow, as seen in Fig. 2-7.

Fig. 2-7 Mini sachets.

MINI SACK SACHET

2 6″ × 4½″ rectangles pink satin
2 ft ¼″-wide pink satin picot-edge ribbon
9″ length 2½″-wide lace ruffle

Poly stuffing
Potpourri or concentrated liquid scent

1. With right sides together, stitch along one 6″ side of the satin rectangles. Press the seam. Pin the lace ruffle to the top edge of the sack, with right sides together and raw edges even. Stitch. Turn the seam to the inside to the sack, press and topstitch.

2. Fold the sack right sides together and pin along the raw edges. Stitch along these edges, sewing the lace ruffle ends together as well. Trim the seam, turn and press.

3. Stuff with poly stuffing and add either potpourri or concentrated liquid scent. Gather the top of the sack and tie with the ribbon. Knot the ends of the ribbon.

DOVE SACHET

12″-×-7″ piece white satin
8″ lengths ⅝″-wide doubleface satin
   ribbon: pink, yellow, blue, and lilac
Poly stuffing

Potpourri or concentrated liquid scent
Craft glue
Disappearing ink pen

1. Fold the satin so that the right sides are together. Place the dove pattern on it and trace the outline with the disappearing ink pen. Stitch along this line leaving open between the dots. Trim the seam, turn and press.

2. Stuff with poly stuffing and potpourri or a few drops of concentrated scent on a cotton ball. Slip stitch the opening closed.

3. Make 4 ribbon roses using the 8″ lengths of satin ribbon, securing them with thread (see instructions in Chapter 5). Glue these to the dove as shown in Fig. 2-7.

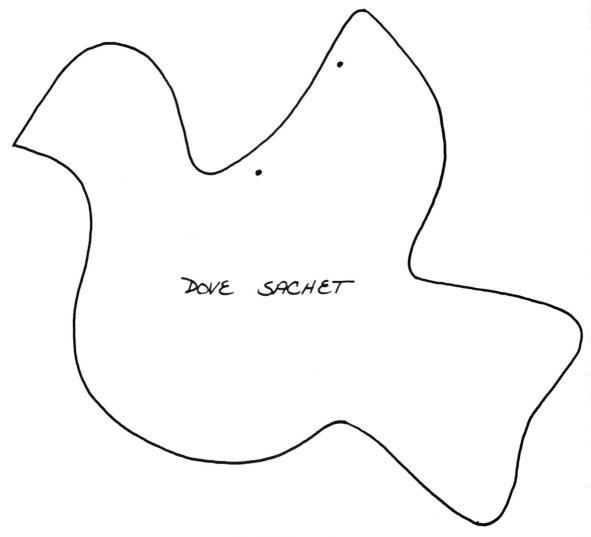

DOVE SACHET

Fig. 2-8 Dove pattern.

BUTTERFLY SACHET

12"-×-6" piece lilac satin
15" length ¼"-wide lilac satin ribbon
8" length ⅝" wide pink doubleface satin
   ribbon

Poly stuffing
Potpourri or concentrated liquid scent
Glue
Disappearing ink pen

1. Fold the satin fabric so that right sides are together. Place the butterfly pattern on it and trace the outline with the disappearing ink pen. Stitch along this line, leaving open between the dots. Trim the seam, turn and press.

2. Stuff with poly stuffing and potpourri or a few drops of concentrated liquid scent. Slip stitch the opening closed.

3. Tie a bow of the ¼" pink ribbon around the center of the butterfly as shown in Fig. 2-7. Make a folded ribbon rose out of the ⅝" wide satin ribbon (see Chapter 5). Secure with thread and glue into place.

Special Ideas For Giving

he bride isn't the only one who wants to remember her wedding day—the bridesmaids deserve mementos too! Make these cute little mini sachets out of fabric that coordinates with each of the bridesmaid's dresses. Embroider each one's name, the names of the bride and groom, and the wedding date onto the back of the sachets. Find out what each bridesmaid's favorite perfume is and scent the sachets accordingly. A bottle of this perfume along with the appropriate sachet will make a lovely thank-you gift for the bride to give to her attendants.

Fig. 2-9 Butterfly pattern.

« Heart Picture Frame »

2 8"-×-10" rectangles ⅛" thick mat board
1 2¼" × 8" rectangle ⅛" thick mat board
40" white heart lace trim, ¾" wide
⅓ yd 45" wide floral print fabric
24" × 20" piece poly batting

Doubleface tape
12 ⅛"-thick mounting squares
Heavy duty craft knife
Disappearing ink pen
Craft glue

1. Trace the heart (Fig. 2-11) onto one piece of mat board 2" up from the bottom and centered. Cut out, leaving a heart-shaped hole in the board.

2. Cut two 8"-×-10" pieces of batting, cut out a heart shape to match the mat board, and glue the two pieces of batting to the front of the board. Cut two more 8" × 10" pieces of batting and glue to the back of the other mat board.

3. Measure 2" down from one end of the 2¼"-×-8" mat board and score with the craft knife. Cut a 9"-×-5" rectangle of fabric and sew right sides together on 3 sides using a ¼" seam. Trim, turn and press. Slip this over the scored mat board with the scored end by the opening. Turn under the excess fabric and slip stitch closed. This forms the stand for the frame.

Fig. 2-10 Heart picture frame.

Fig. 2-11 Heart pattern for picture frame.

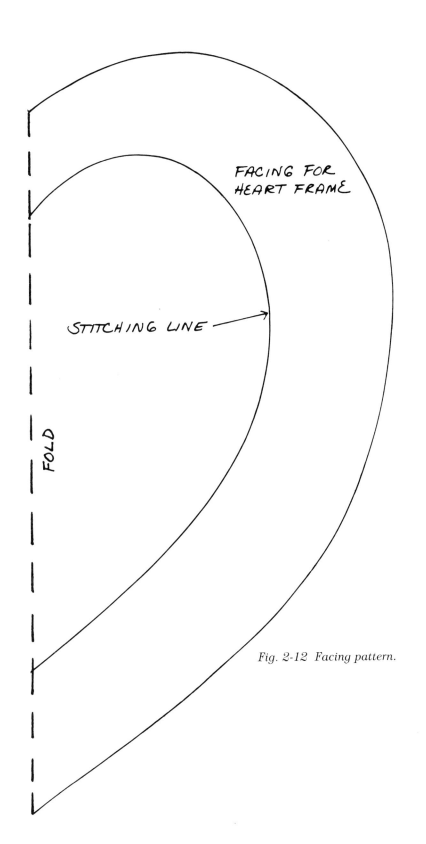

FACING FOR
HEART FRAME

STITCHING LINE

FOLD

Fig. 2-12 Facing pattern.

4. Cut out a piece of fabric measuring 10″ × 12″. Using Fig. 2-12, make a complete heart facing pattern as described for the Heart Box, page 10. Cut out one heart facing from fabric. Place the heart facing over the fabric rectangle right sides together, placing the point of the heart 1½″ up from the bottom edge of the rectangle. Stitch on the stitching line. Cut out the center of the heart. Trim the seam, clip the curves. Turn the facing to the inside and press.

5. Place doubleface tape on the mat side of the heart-shaped mat board. Stretch the assembled fabric piece over the batting side and secure to the tape to form the front of the heart frame, stretching the heart facing to the back as well. Glue on the trim ½″ in from all edges.

6. Cut a second piece of fabric measuring 10″ × 12″. Place doublefaced tape on the mat side of the back of the frame and stretch the fabric over the batting to form the back of the frame. Place 4 mounting squares on each side and the top of the frame. Set the frame front on the squares and press. Glue the stand to the back of the frame. Slip in a picture through the open bottom of the frame.

Special Ideas For Giving

This heart picture frame is your chance to display your photographic skills! Take that perfect picture you snapped at the happy couple's wedding and have it enlarged to fit the frame. Or, search through your photo album and collect as many shots of them you can find. Have these enlarged and write a little note on the back of each one to bring to mind the joy of that moment. Put the pictures in chronological order and slip them into the frame. You have just provided the "lovebirds" with a unique history of their courtship!

« Potpourri Travel Roll-up Bag »

Tissue or pattern paper
13"-×-19" rectangle pink lace
13"-×-19" rectangle white organza
13"-×-19" rectangle poly batting
13"-×-36" piece white eyelet fabric
Potpourri

1 yd $\frac{1}{2}$"-wide pink satin picot-edge
  ribbon
4 small white Velcro dots fasteners
2 ft 1$\frac{1}{2}$"-wide white lace ruffle
5 ft white double-fold bias tape

1. Using Fig. 2-15 as a guide, make a pattern for the roll-up bag from tissue paper. The pattern will be a rectangle 12" x 18" with rounded corners at one end.

2. Using the pattern, cut one lace, one organza, one batting, and one eyelet shape. From the remaining eyelet, cut one 12" x 5" rectangle for the small pocket and one 12" x 9$\frac{1}{4}$" rectangle for the large pocket. Set these aside.

3. Place the large eyelet piece right side facing down. Place the batting piece on top of this. Sprinkle the batting with potpourri. Place the organza over this. Place the lace right side facing up on top of all of them. Keeping these sections flat so that the potpourri doesn't fall out, pin along the edges and

Fig. 2-13 Potpourri travel roll-up bag.

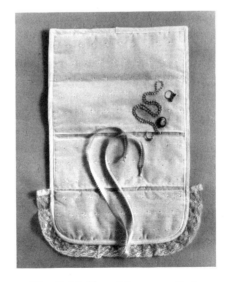

Fig. 2-14 Travel bag, unrolled.

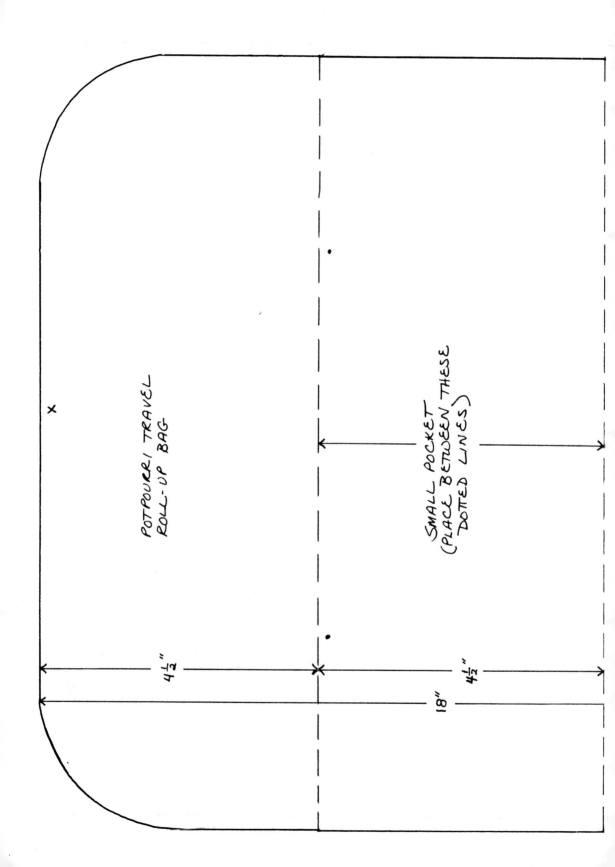

POTPOURRI TRAVEL
ROLL-UP BAG

SMALL POCKET
(PLACE BETWEEN THESE
DOTTED LINES)

X

$4\frac{1}{2}$"

$4\frac{1}{2}$"

18"

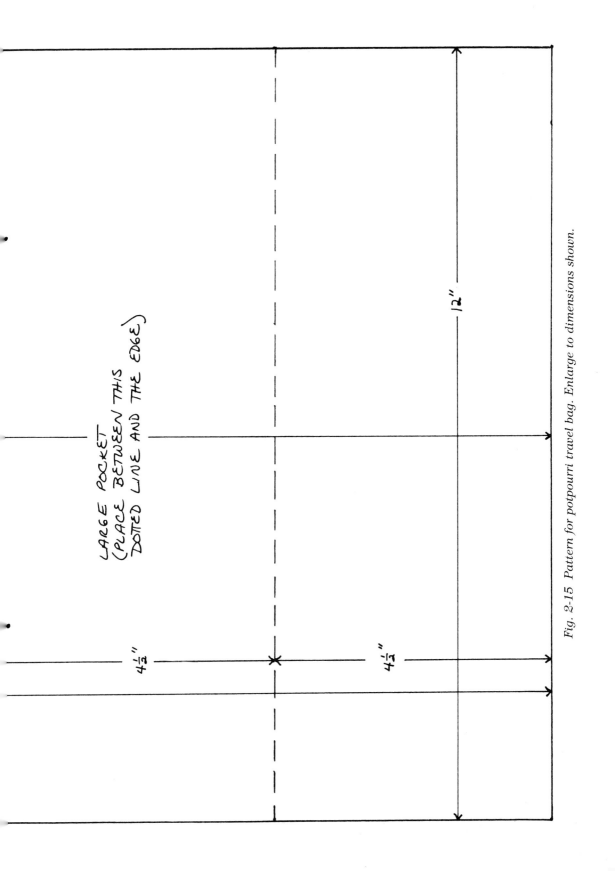

LARGE POCKET
(PLACE BETWEEN THIS
DOTTED LINE AND THE EDGE)

4½"

4½"

12"

Fig. 2-15 Pattern for potpourri travel bag. Enlarge to dimensions shown.

baste. Keeping the fabric flat, stitch across the fabric at $4\frac{1}{2}''$ intervals, as indicated by the dotted line in Fig. 2-15.

4. Turn under $\frac{1}{4}''$ along both long sides of the small pocket and topstitch. Turn under $\frac{1}{4}''$ along the top edge of the large pocket and topstitch.

5. Pin the pockets into place. Baste along the outside edges. Stitch along the bottom edge of the smaller pocket, following the dotted line.

6. Bind all edges with bias tape. Trim the curved end with lace ruffle, starting at the top dotted line and turning under the ruffle ends $\frac{1}{2}''$. Fold the ribbon in half and sew to the X. Knot the ribbon ends. Sew on the Velcro dots in the four spots indicated in Fig. 2-15.

Special Ideas for Giving

What a perfect time to give the bride a travel bag—just in time for the honeymoon! Make it to match her wedding dress, perhaps using some of the lace that was used to make her dress. If possible, save some flowers from the wedding and use these to make a potpourri to sprinkle under the lace. (Follow the potpourri instructions in Chapter 5.) You may want to embroider the bride's new full name onto an inside pocket along with her wedding date. And if you're feeling especially generous, slip a little piece of jewelry into one of the pockets as well, perhaps that heirloom of Grandma's that she has always loved.

« Scented Padded Hanger »

Wooden hanger 17" across
15" piece 1⅜"-wide pink organza ribbon
  (or organza fabric cut on the bias)
Potpourri
9" piece 30-gauge wrapping wire
2 strips poly batting, 2" × 30"

2 ft ½"-wide pink satin picot-edge ribbon
2 ft ½"-wide pink satin doubleface
  ribbon
Craft glue
2 10"-×-2½" rectangles pink lace
4 10"-×-2½" rectangles lilac satin

1. Place one lace rectangle over the right side of one satin rectangle. Place the other satin rectangle on top of this right sides together. Stitch around three sides leaving one short end open. Trim the seam, turn and press. Make a second piece just like this one.

2. Fold one end of the satin picot-edge ribbon over the tip of the metal section of the hanger, securing with glue. When the glue is dry, wrap the ribbon around the metal section, overlapping the ribbon to cover the metal completely and placing small dots of glue along the underside of the ribbon to further secure it. Loop the end of the ribbon around the wooden part of the hanger and tie, cutting off any excess.

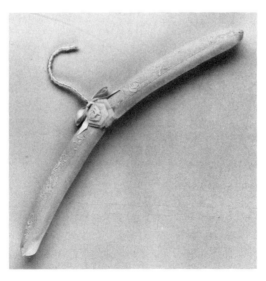

Fig. 2-16 Scented padded hanger.

3. Spread a layer of glue over one strip of batting and sprinkle with potpourri. Place the other strip of batting over this one and let the glue dry.

4. Spread glue on the wooden hanger. Starting at the base of the hook, glue one end of the batting strip down. Fold the strip around the wooden section of the hanger, stretching slightly so that the other end of the strip ends again at the base of the hook. Let dry.

5. Cover each side of the padded hanger with the lace and satin pieces. Sew these pieces together at the base of the hook.

6. Tie the center of the doubleface satin ribbon to the base of the hook. Loop the ribbon around the padded section to cover the seam and tie again at the hook. Tie the remaining ribbon in a bow.

7. Following the instructions for the folded ribbon rose (see Chapter 5), make a pink rose and glue under the bow.

Special Ideas for Giving

The wedding dress and beautiful negligee are two wonderful elements of every bride's wedding. Wouldn't it be nice if the bride had an equally beautiful hanger for them? If it is possible to obtain fabric to match the wedding dress, use it for the hanger. Choose ribbon for the bow and rose that matches the bridesmaids' dresses. You may want to embroider the names of the bride and groom and their wedding date onto the back of the hanger to make it a real memento. Just for fun, attach a small bottle of the bride's favorite perfume to the hanger near the rose for the bride to use on her special day.

3

GIFTS FOR A BABY

« Teddy Bear Birth Announcement »

11" square Aida cloth (11 squares per inch)
8"-diameter wooden embroidery hoop
Embroidery floss: pink, yellow, light blue, light brown, and black
Blunt-tipped embroidery needle
10" ½"-wide pink satin picot-edge ribbon
1 ft ⅛"-wide pink and light blue satin ribbon to match floss

18" ⅛"-wide yellow satin ribbon to match floss
Craft glue
2½ ft 1½"-wide teddy bear embroidered ruffle
Graph paper

Fig. 3-1 Teddy bear birth announcement.

1. Place the Aida cloth in the hoop. Follow the bear and balloon outlines in Fig. 3-2 to embroider as follows: Bear body—light brown; bear tummy, ears, and feet—pink; bear eyes, nose, and foot dots—black; top balloon—light blue; middle balloon—yellow; bottom balloon—pink.

2. Backstitch bear's mouth and eyes in black. Backstitch the bear's pink feet in light brown.

3. Use the ABC chart and separate piece of graph paper to plan out the name, date, and weight of your baby. Embroider in black backstitch, centering the information in the balloons.

4. Cut a 6″ length of each color $\frac{1}{8}$″-wide ribbons and tie together in a knot. Glue this to the bear's hand. Trim the ribbon to reach the balloons and glue to the balloons. With the remaining $\frac{1}{8}$″ ribbon, make 2 yellow bows, 1 pink bow and 1 blue bow. Glue into place at the base of the balloons and at the bear's neck.

5. Recenter the Aida cloth in the hoop if necessary, placing the screw at the top of the hoop. Trim the Aida cloth to leave $\frac{1}{2}$″ excess beyond the hoop. Glue this excess cloth down to the back of the hoop. Glue the ruffle to the back of the hoop. Make a bow out of the $\frac{1}{2}$″-wide pink ribbon and glue to the screw at the top of the hoop.

Special Ideas for Giving

he teddy bear birth announcement is already custom made, having the baby's name, birthdate and birth weight embroidered onto it already. But why not add another personal touch by attaching a special photograph to the back of the hoop? This photo could be one you took of the happy parents and the newborn at the hospital or at home. Another idea is to attach baby photos of the parents along with the newborn's picture. This way, when anyone asks "Who does the baby look like?", you can just remove the birth announcement from the wall and let the inquisitive person decide for himself!

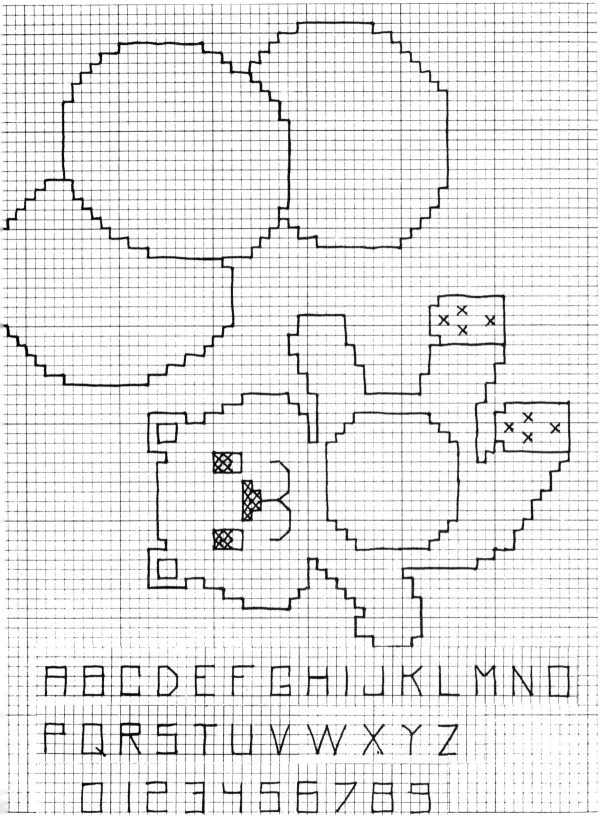

Fig. 3-2 Embroidery chart for birth announcement.

« Lace Baby Quilt and Pillow »

Directions for this quilt are given based on a lace fabric made up of $5\frac{3}{4}''$ squares. If you use lace fabric with squares of a different size, alter your quilt dimensions accordingly.

5 ft 45"-wide ivory cotton chintz
1 yd 45"-wide lace square fabric
6 yd ¼"-wide pink satin picot-edge
  ribbon
Quilt batting

5 yd 5"-wide white eyelet ruffle
White strong thread (buttonhole
  weight)
Long needle with large eye

   1. Cut the lace fabric into a rectangular piece, measuring 5 squares by 6 squares (approximately 34" x 28"). Cut two rectangular pieces of chintz to match.
   2. Baste the wrong side of the lace to the right side of one rectangle of chintz. Pin the eyelet ruffle to this lace piece, right sides together, with the raw ends of the ruffle meeting in the center of the bottom. Fold in an inch of

Fig. 3-3 Lace baby quilt.

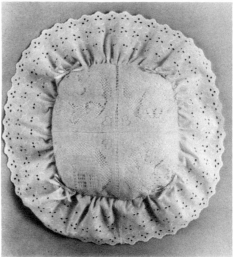

Fig. 3-4 Lace pillow.

extra ruffle at each corner. Sew the ruffle ends together using a $\frac{1}{4}''$ seam. Press the seam and topstitch. Baste around all edges.

3. Place the second chintz rectangle over the lace, right sides together and pin. Stitch around all sides, using a $\frac{1}{2}''$ seam and leaving a 12″ opening at the bottom. Trim the seam. Do not turn right side out yet.

4. Depending upon desired thickness, cut 2 or 3 layers of quilt batting to size. Lay these out flat on top of each other and place the chintz/lace rectangle over them. Pin. Stitch, following the original sewing line, leaving open again at the bottom. Trim, turn and steam lightly. Slip stitch the opening closed.

5. Using the long needle and strong thread, tack at the corners of each square, sewing through all thicknesses. Use 8″ of ribbon to make bows. Sew these into place at the corners of each square.

6. To make the pillow, cut a 4-square piece of lace and 2 squares of chintz to match. Round all the corners. Sew the lace, chintz, and remaining eyelet ruffle together as for the quilt, leaving open 6″ along the bottom edge. Trim the seam, turn right side out and steam lightly. Stuff with pieces of quilt batting. Slip stitch the opening closed. Make 4 bows as for the quilt and sew to the 4 corners of the pillow.

Special Ideas for Giving

e sure to choose the proper color of bows for this quilt—pink or blue! Or, color coordinate the quilt to match the baby's room. Does the mother have a favorite nursery rhyme or lullabye she sings to her new-born? If so, why not embroider it into the back of the quilt? It will make a happy memory when the child is grown. Perhaps, because of your thoughtful gift, the same lullabye will be sung to the grown child's own baby when he or she is born. What a nice family tradition to start!

« Crib Hearts »

2 yd ½"-wide white ruffled lace
2 yd ⅝"-wide yellow satin ribbon
4"-×-8" remnants calico fabric in the

colors of the rainbow: red, orange,
yellow, green, blue, and purple
Poly stuffing

1. Using the crib heart pattern (Fig. 3-6), cut out 2 hearts from each color of calico. Sew the lace ruffle right sides together close to the edges of one of the hearts. Pin the matching heart onto this one, right sides together. Stitch using a ¼" seam, leaving open between the dots.
2. Trim the seam, clip the curves, turn right side out, press, stuff and slip stitch the opening closed. Make the other 5 hearts in the same way.
3. Stitch the hearts together by hand at the lace borders, placing the colors of the hearts in the order of the rainbow. Cut the ribbon in half. Fold each piece in half and sew onto each end for ties.

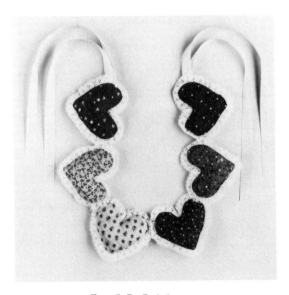

Fig. 3-5 Crib hearts.

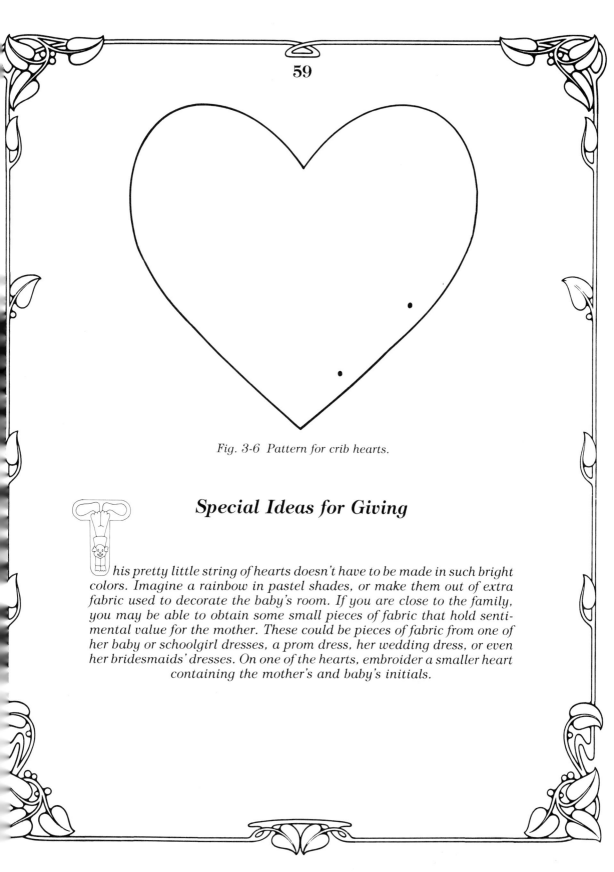

Fig. 3-6 Pattern for crib hearts.

Special Ideas for Giving

This pretty little string of hearts doesn't have to be made in such bright colors. Imagine a rainbow in pastel shades, or make them out of extra fabric used to decorate the baby's room. If you are close to the family, you may be able to obtain some small pieces of fabric that hold sentimental value for the mother. These could be pieces of fabric from one of her baby or schoolgirl dresses, a prom dress, her wedding dress, or even her bridesmaids' dresses. On one of the hearts, embroider a smaller heart containing the mother's and baby's initials.

« Heart Doll »

½ yd 60"-wide pink stretch terry fabric
Red and black #5 DMC embroidery
   thread
Large eye embroidery needle
4"-diameter embroidery hoop
Poly stuffing

Disappearing ink pen
Craft glue
1 yd ½"-wide pink satin ribbon
2 yd hot pink yarn
4" square hot pink felt

1. Make paper patterns as shown in Fig. 3-8. Cut the terry fabric in half. Place one piece on top of the other, right sides together so that the nap is running in the same direction. Pin the pattern pieces onto the fabric so that the nap is running down. Cutting through both pieces of fabric at once, cut out 1 heart shape, 2 arms, and 2 legs.

2. Right sides together, sew 2 arm pieces together, using a ¼" seam and leaving open between the dots. Trim the seams, clip the curves, turn right side out, and press. Sew another arm and 2 legs the same way.

Fig. 3-7 Heart doll.

3. Embroider the mouth and eyes on the face of the doll. Cut out 2 cheek hearts from the felt and glue into position.

4. Pin the arms and legs to the right side of the face heart, placing them between the Xs. Place the other heart over this right sides together and pin. Make sure all the arms and legs are tucked in away from the stitching line and that the thumbs point up and the toes point out. Stitch using a $\frac{1}{4}''$ seam, leaving open between the dots. Trim the seam, clip the curves, turn right side out and press.

5. Stuff the arms, legs, and body. Slip stitch the openings closed. Using the disappearing ink pen, mark the lines on the insides of the hands. Sew the lines to each other by hand, making the doll's hands "cup." Sew through all thicknesses at the x mark on the legs to form knees.

6. Wrap the yarn around the fingers of one hand and tie the yarn ends together to form the hair. Sew to the top of the head. Make 2 bows out of the ribbon and sew to the tops of the feet.

Special Ideas for Giving

This soft cuddly doll will be Baby's first love affair—after Mom and Dad, of course! He looks so loving, you just have to embroider the words "I LOVE YOU (baby's name)" across the back. You may want to embroider the baby's birthdate as well. For a humorous twist, combine the Heart Doll with a gift of clothing for the baby, by dressing the doll in the baby's new outfit! Wouldn't he look sweet in lace booties and bonnet?

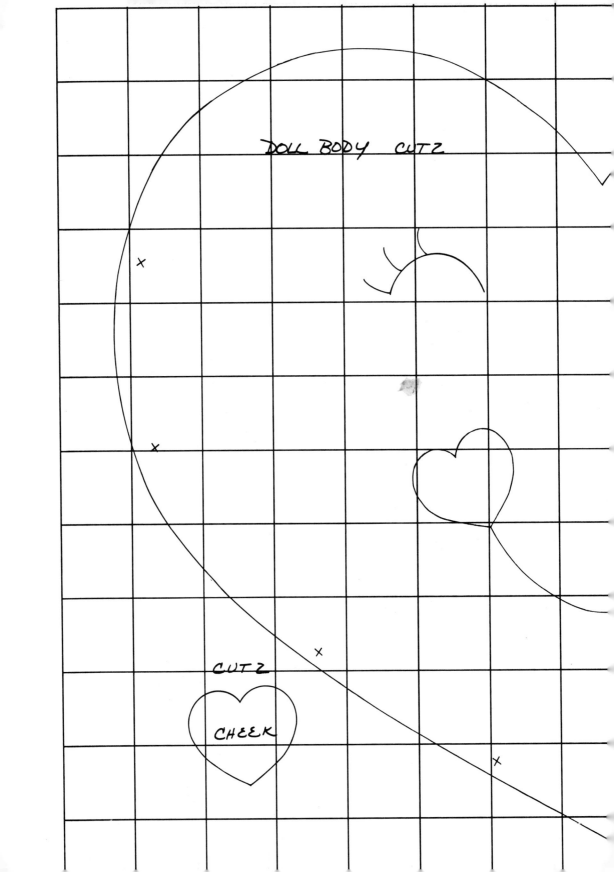

DOLL BODY CUTZ

CUTZ

CHEEK

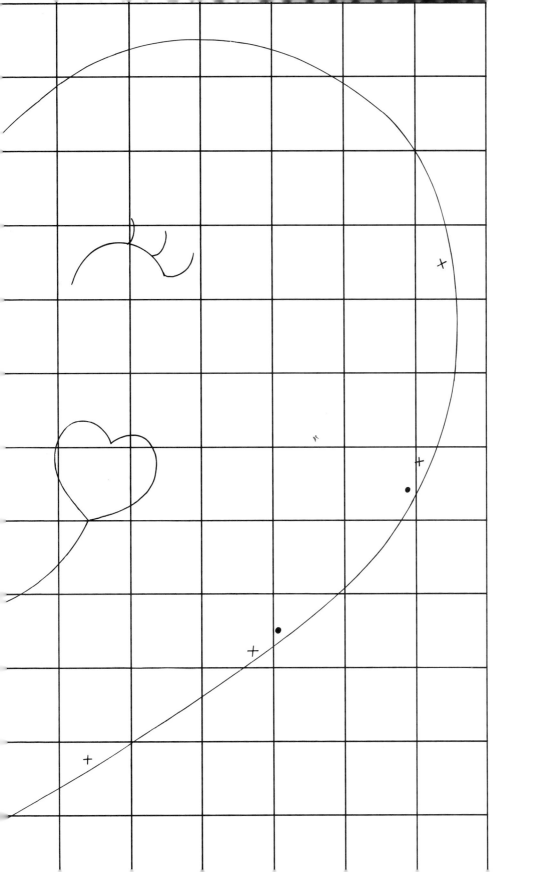

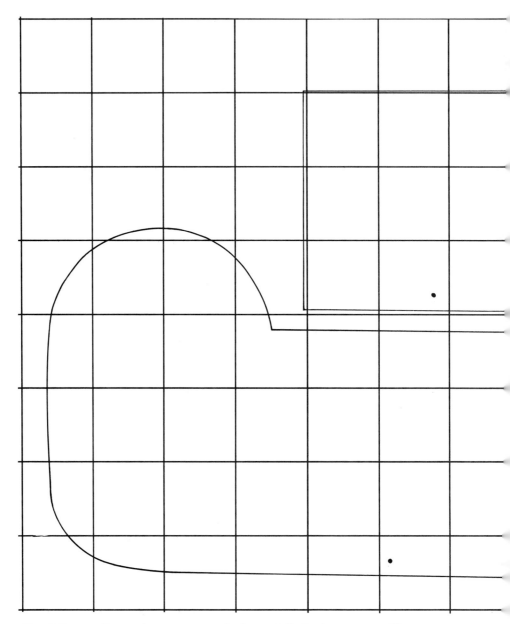

Fig. 3-8 cont. Leg and arm patterns for heart doll. Each square = 1".

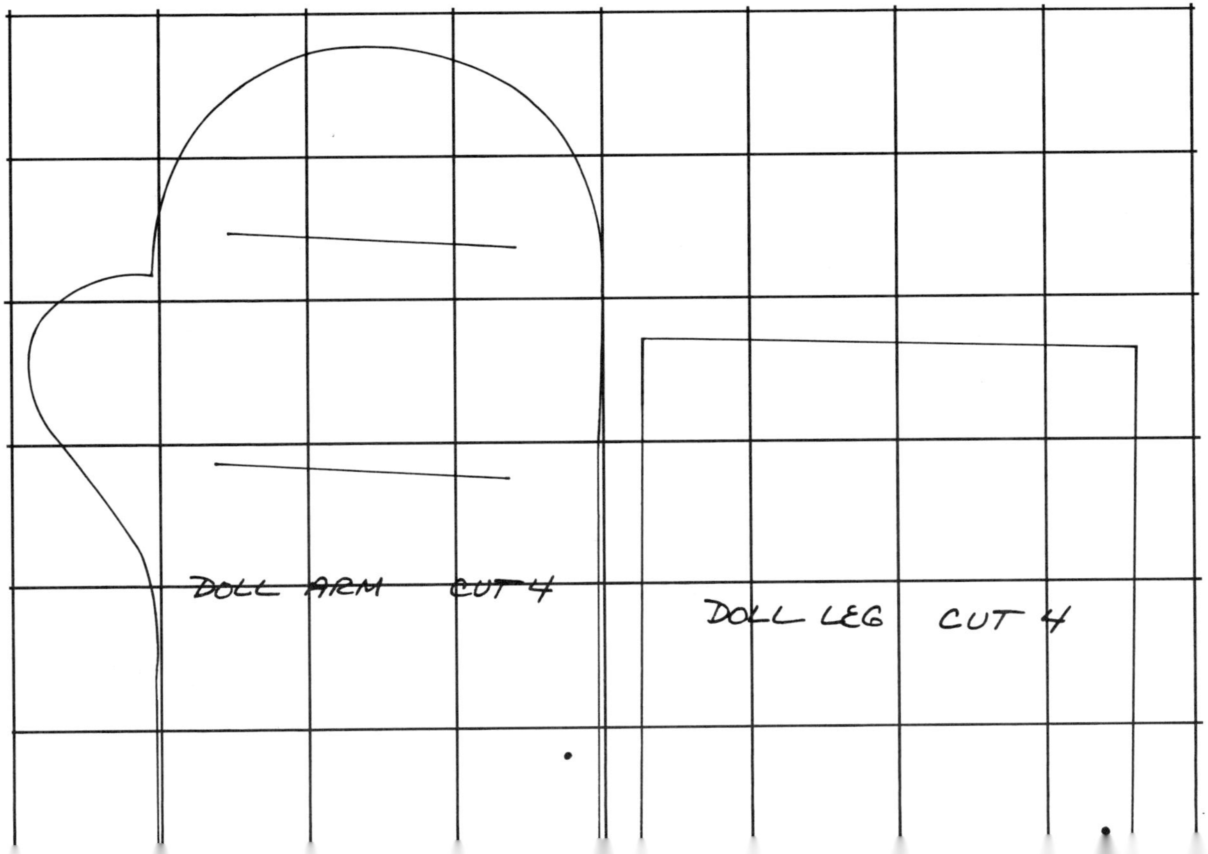

DOLL ARM CUT 4

DOLL LEG CUT 4

« Baby Bib with Chicken Scratch Heart »

$\frac{1}{3}$ yd 45"-wide lavender gingham (9 by
   10 squares per inch)
$1\frac{1}{4}$ yd 1"-wide white ruffled eyelet
White and purple embroidery floss
4" embroidery hoop

Embroidery needle
1 yd $\frac{1}{4}$"-wide white satin picot-edge
   ribbon
Disappearing ink pen

    1. Enlarge patterns. Draw the outline of the bib pocket (Fig. 3-10) onto a piece of gingham, but do not cut out. Place into the embroidery hoop and embroider the chicken scratch heart design (Fig. 3-11), centering the heart. (Be sure to match the squares-per-inch diagram.)
    2. Cut out the pocket. Cut out a second pocket and 2 bib pieces (Fig. 3-12), making sure the gingham matches the squares-per-inch diagram on the pattern pieces.
    3. Turn under $\frac{1}{4}$" on the ruffle ends and pin right sides and raw edges together along the embroidered pocket. Baste close to the edge. Pin the other

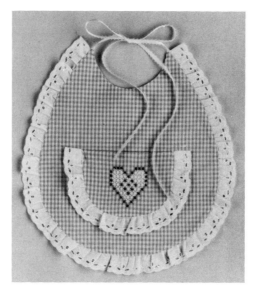

Fig. 3-9 Baby bib with chicken scratch heart.

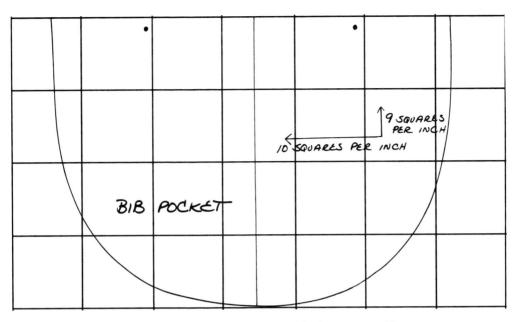

Fig. 3-10 Pattern for bib pocket. Each square = 1".

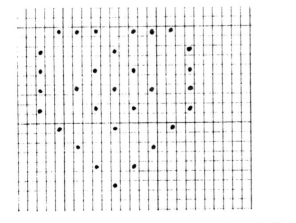

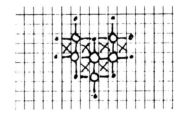

Fig. 3-11 Design for chicken scratch heart (left) and sample of chicken scratch fill-in (right).

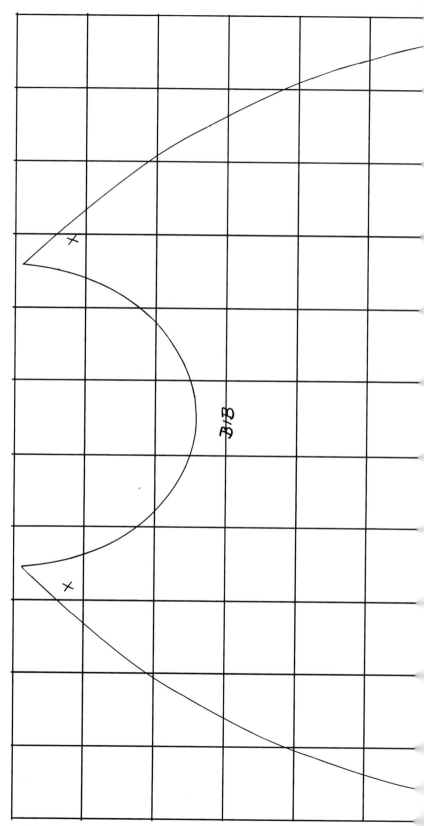

Fig. 3-12 Bib pattern.
Each square = 1".

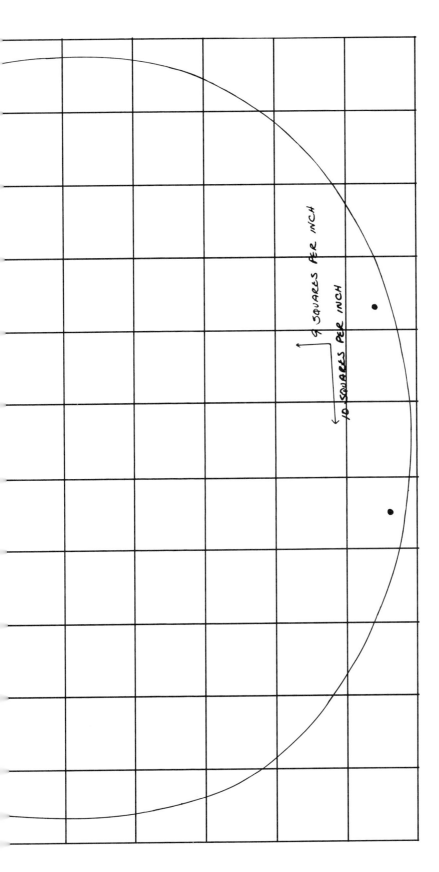

9 SQUARES PER INCH

10 SQUARES PER INCH

pocket over this and stitch using a $\frac{1}{4}''$ seam and leaving open between the dots. Trim the seam, clip the curves, turn right side out and press. Slip stitch the opening closed.

4. Turn under $\frac{1}{4}''$ on the ruffle ends and pin right sides and raw edges together along the edges of the bib front, starting and ending the ruffle at the Xs. Finish turn and press as you did the pocket. Slip stitch the opening closed. Center the pocket on the bib and stitch close to the edge. Sew $\frac{1}{2}$ yd ribbbon onto each side for the bib ties.

Special Ideas for Giving

s there an heirloom silver baby spoon that has been handed down in your family? This bib with its cute heart pocket provides the perfect "wrapping" for such an important gift. Of course, if an heirloom spoon isn't available, there are other wonderful surprises to tuck into the bib pocket. A silver rattle, a small frame with baby's first photo in it, or a gold baby bracelet are a few lovely gifts that come to mind. Or, start the silver spoon tradition by furnishing one of your own choice.

« Bib with Bunny Toy »

½ yd 36"-wide pink gingham fabric
3 yd pink narrow double-fold bias tape
10" square white stretch terry fabric
1 ft ¼"-wide black velvet ribbon
1"-diameter white pom-pom

Embroidery floss: pink, blue and black
Poly stuffing
Embroidery needle
Disappearing ink pen
Craft glue

1. Make a paper pattern as shown in Fig. 3-14. To make the bib, cut out two bib shapes and one bib pocket (a rectangle 8" x 5¼") from the gingham. Stitch the shoulder seams, press and topstitch.

2. Cut one bib shape up the center to form the two back pieces. Turn under ¼" along these cut edges, press and topstitch. Bind all the outside raw edges with bias tape. Use the remaining bias tape to bind the neck edge, centering the tape so that the excess forms two ties. Knot the ends.

3. To make the pocket, turn under ¼" along the top edge, press and topstitch. Press under ¼" along the other three edges. Center the pocket on the bib front 2" from the bottom. Topstitch along the side and bottom edges.

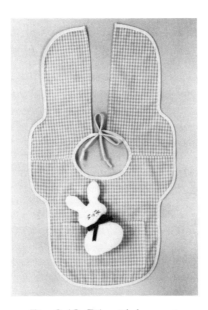

Fig. 3-13 Bib with bunny toy.

4. To make the bunny, fold the terry fabric in half, right sides together. Place the pattern on the fabric so that the nap is running down. Trace around the pattern with the disappearing ink pen. Stitch along this line, leaving a $1\frac{1}{2}''$ opening at the bottom. Stitch a second time. Trim close to the stitching line. Turn right side out and press.

5. To finish the bunny, stuff and slip stitch the opening closed. Glue on the pom-pom tail. Draw the face markings onto the bunny face using the disappearing ink pen. Embroider a pink nose using a satin stitch, a pink mouth using a backstitch, blue eyes using a satin stitch, and black whiskers using a long stitch. Tie a bow around the neck and place in the bib pocket.

Special Ideas for Giving

ere's a bib any mother will love—a bib with a built-in toy for amusement! Baby will look forward to mealtimes with his little bunny friend. You may want to embroider the baby's name onto the back of the bunny. Or perhaps you can find a cute dish and cup decorated with bunnies to accompany the baby's new "dinner outfit." Another idea is to put together a baby food "care" package from the local gourmet store. Buy all the fun food items like imported teething crackers or English porridge mix that the mother would never go out and buy herself. Both Baby and Mom will be happy to have a little change from their usual mealtime routine!

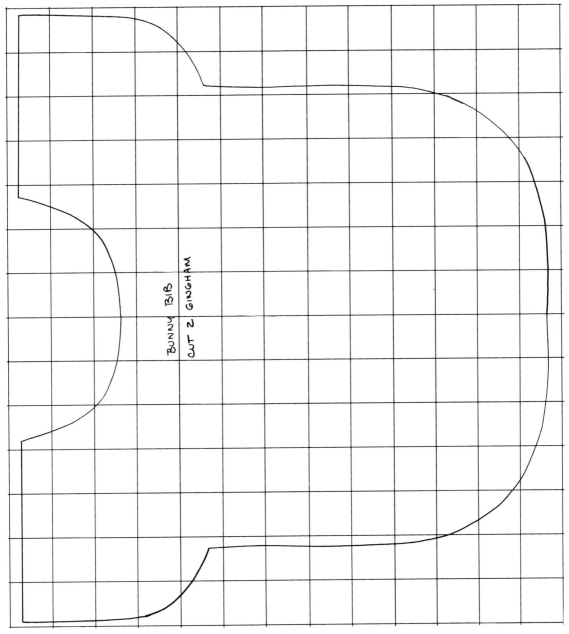

BUNNY BIB

CUT 2 GINGHAM

Fig. 3-14 Bunny bib pattern. Each square = 1".

BUNNY

TRACE ONTO
WHITE STRETCH
TERRY

Fig. 3-14 cont. Bunny pattern. Use size shown.

BUNNY BIB POCKET
CUT 1 GINGHAM

Fig. 3-14 cont. Bib pocket pattern.

« Baby Jars with Chicken Scratch Heart Lids »

*7" square gingham (9 by 10 squares
per inch) in red, lavender, and mint
green
1 ft ¼"-wide satin picot-edge ribbon in
red, lavender, and mint green
Embroidery floss: white, red, mint
green, and purple
4" embroidery hoop
Embroidery needle*

*3 Mason jars with lids and rings (3"
mouth × 5" tall)
Poly stuffing
Cardboard
White enamel spray paint
Craft glue
2 yd 1¼"-wide white lace ruffle
Disappearing ink pen*

   1. Find center of gingham squares and place into hoop. Embroider, following chicken scratch double heart chart (Fig. 3-16). (Note: Embroider so that the 10 squares per inch runs from right to left and the 9 squares per inch runs from top to bottom.)

   2. Trim the square into a 6½"-diameter circle, with the embroidery centered. Place the lace ruffle right sides and raw edges together around the edge of the

Fig. 3-15 Baby jars with heart lids.

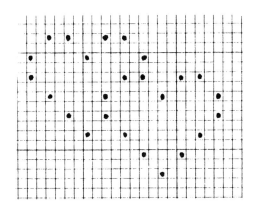

Fig. 3-16 Embroidery design for chicken scratch hearts.

circle and pin, turning under $\frac{1}{4}''$ on the ruffle ends. Stitch using a $\frac{1}{4}''$ seam. Turn seam under, press and topstitch.

3. Spray paint jar lids white. Let dry. Glue ribbon trim on. Cut out 3 cardboard circles to match the lids. Place a small amount of poly filling on the carboard circle, place the embroidered gingham circle over this and push into the ring. Smooth out any folds. Place the jar lid on the jar and screw on the decorated jar ring.

Special Ideas for Giving

A new mother needs a lot of things, including time for herself! Here's a creative gift to pamper the new mother with. Fill two of the jars with normal baby things, such as pacifiers or cotton swabs. Then fill the third jar with little paper hearts on which you've written thoughtful IOUs. Take them from the following list, or use your imagination to make up your own.

IOU one lunch at the restaurant of your choice!

IOU one trip to the hair dresser!

IOU one evening of babysitting!

IOU one afternoon movie!

IOU one manicure!

GIFTS FOR CHILDREN

« Heart Tooth Fairy Pillow »

5" square white felt
24"-×-30" piece heart-print red flannel
1 yd 1"-wide eyelet ruffle

24"-×-30" piece poly batting
Poly stuffing
Disappearing ink pen

1. Using Fig. 4-2, make a complete pattern and enlarge; cut 2 hearts out of fabric and batting. Use the tooth pattern to cut out a felt tooth.

2. Place the batting on the back of the hearts and baste close to the edges.

Fig. 4-1 Heart tooth fairy pillow.

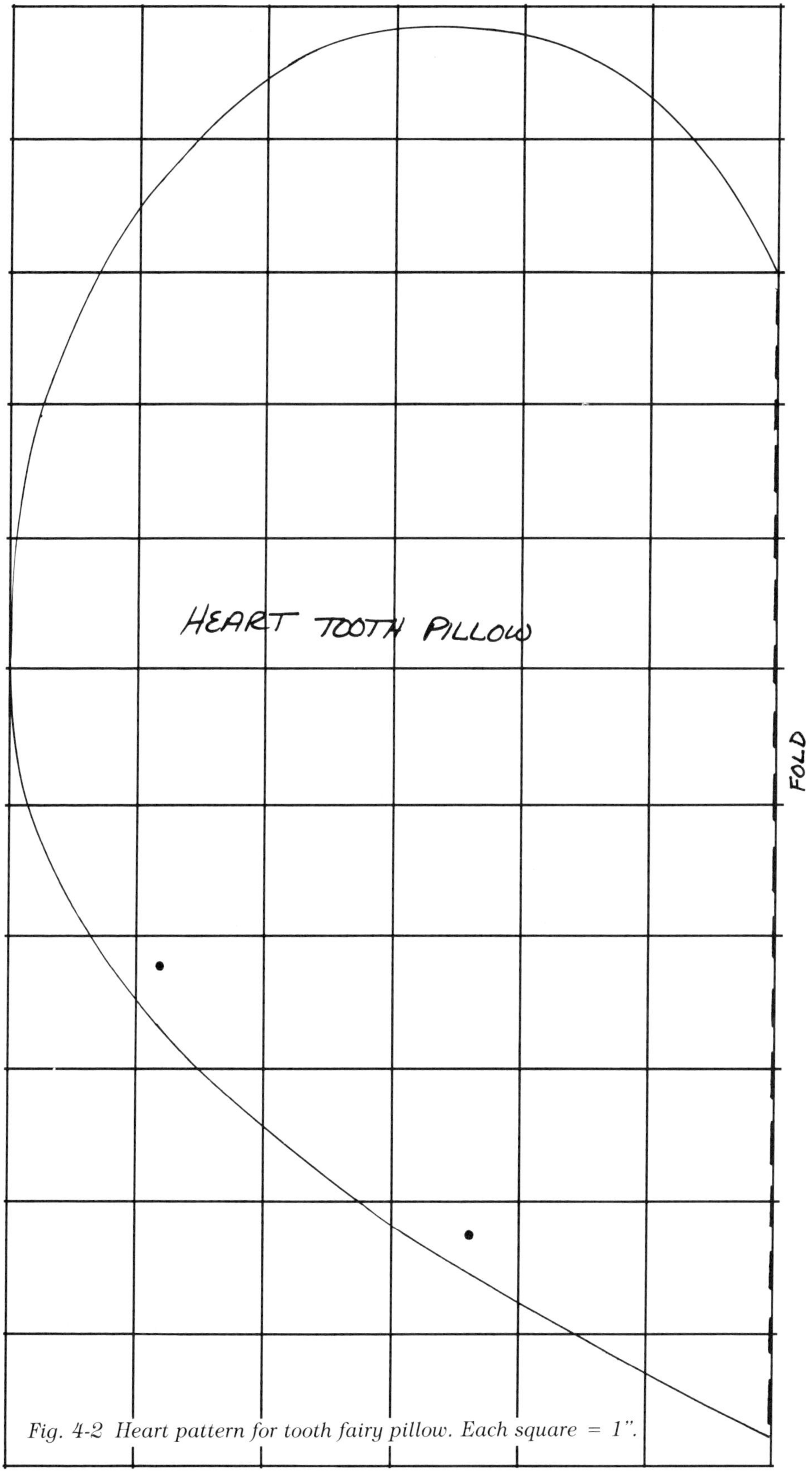

HEART TOOTH PILLOW

FOLD

Fig. 4-2 Heart pattern for tooth fairy pillow. Each square = 1".

Dear _____,

I hear you have a tooth for me! Leave it in this magic pocket and I will fly into your bedroom tonight to get it and leave you a surprise!

I love you,

P.S. Brush your teeth!

Tooth Fairy

TOOTH FOR
TOOTH PILLOW

Fig. 4-2 cont. Tooth pattern for pillow. Use size shown.

Center the felt tooth on one heart and stitch through all thicknesses around the edge of the tooth between the dots to form a pocket.

3. Measure in 1″ from the edge of the pillow front and mark with the disappearing ink pen. Topstitch along this line using white thread. Pin the ruffle to the pillow front, right sides and raw edges together. Baste. Pin the pillow back to the front, right sides together, and stitch using a ¼″ seam, leaving open between the dots.

4. Trim the seam, clip the curves, turn right side out and press. Stuff and slip stitch the opening closed.

Special Ideas for Giving

T he tooth fairy lives! We adults know that, for after all, we each have a mouthful of teeth living on in baby tooth heaven, don't we? But children must be carefully introduced to this mysterious spirit. What fun you will have giving this tooth fairy pillow to the little child in your life who has just lost his first tooth. Cut out a tooth-shaped piece of paper to fit into the pocket, and write a letter to the child from Miss Tooth Fairy herself. And just for fun, tuck in a little feather to show she was really there!

« Circus ABC Counted Cross Stitch Name »

Ecru Aida cloth, 14 squares per inch—
  amount determined by length of
  name to be embroidered
Embroidery floss in various colors
6"-diameter embroidery hoop

Blunt counted cross stitch needle
Frame to fit size of embroidery
Circus ABC counted cross stitch charts
  (Chapter 6)

1. Plan the amount of Aida cloth you will need by counting the number of squares across the letters that make up the name you are embroidering. Add 3 squares for spacing between each letter and 3″ for spacing and framing on each end of the name. Each letter uses 42 squares vertically, so plan the height of the fabric you will need accordingly, leaving 3″ on the top and the bottom for spacing and framing. An 11-square-per-inch Aida cloth will make the name larger, and you will need more cloth. An 18-square-per-inch Aida cloth will make the name smaller and you will need less cloth.

2. Embroider the name, letter by letter, following the chart, and centering the name on the cloth. Press using a pressing cloth. Frame.

Fig. 4-3 Circus ABC counted cross stitch name.

Special Ideas for Giving

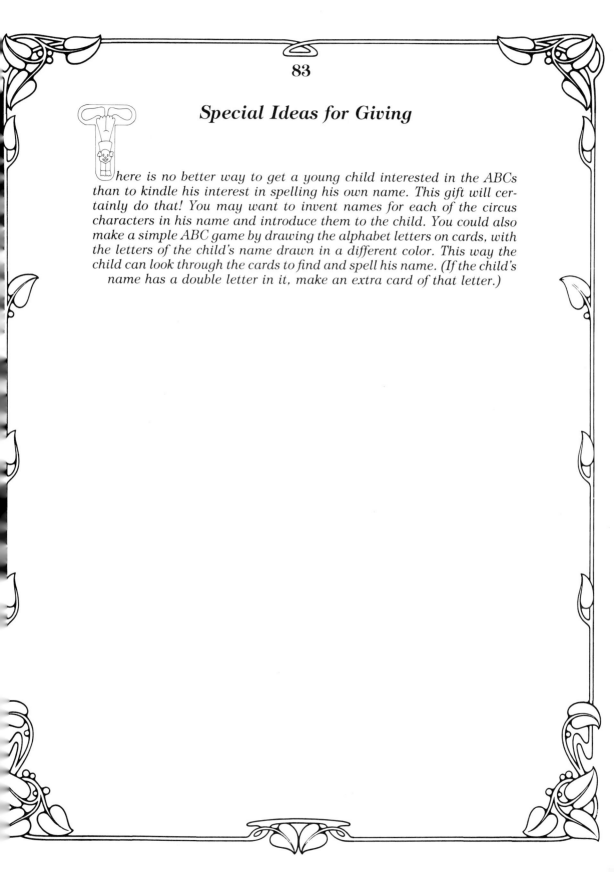

There is no better way to get a young child interested in the ABCs than to kindle his interest in spelling his own name. This gift will certainly do that! You may want to invent names for each of the circus characters in his name and introduce them to the child. You could also make a simple ABC game by drawing the alphabet letters on cards, with the letters of the child's name drawn in a different color. This way the child can look through the cards to find and spell his name. (If the child's name has a double letter in it, make an extra card of that letter.)

« Circus Alphabet Quilt »

13 ft 45"-wide yellow fabric
4½ ft 45"-wide white fabric
60"-×-52" piece quilt batting
18 8-yd skeins crewel yarn in the
    following colors: 2 yellow, 2 royal
    blue, 2 lime green, 2 black, 1 light

orange, 1 orange, 1 flesh, 1 hot pink,
    2 brown, 2 red, 2 light pink
8"-diameter embroidery hoop
Crewel embroidery needle
Water-soluble ink pen
Circus Alphabet outlines (Chapter 6)

    1. Follow the layout pattern for the yellow fabric (Fig. 4-5) to measure and cut two 52" x 30" pieces for the quilt backing, 28 8"-x-8" squares for the quilt front, two 3"-x-56" strips for the top and bottom quilt edgings, and two 3"-x-64" strips for the quilt side edgings.

    2. Follow the layout pattern for the white fabric (Fig. 4-6) to measure 28 8"-x-8" squares for the embroidered sections of the front of the quilt. Draw the squares with pencil, but do not cut them out until all squares have been embroidered.

Fig. 4-4 Circus alphabet quilt.

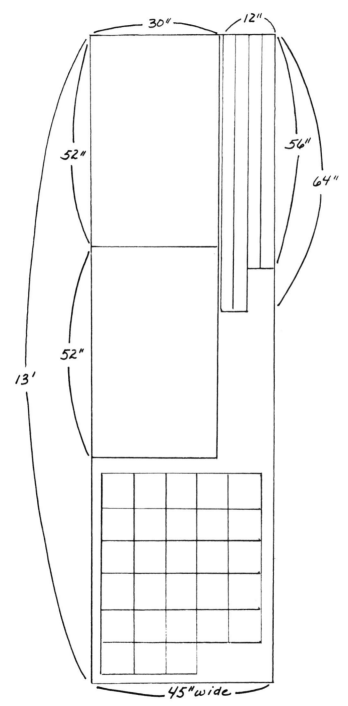

Fig. 4-5 Yellow fabric layout.

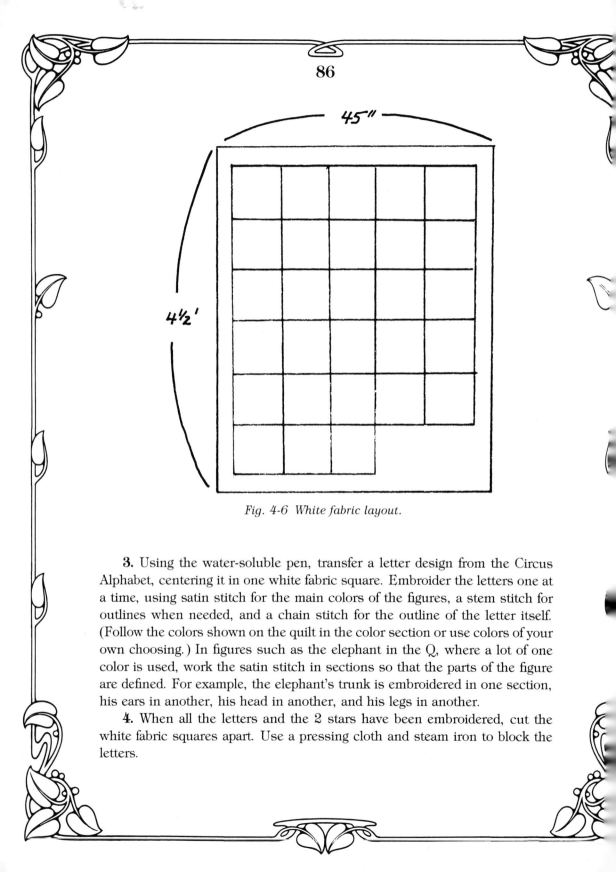

Fig. 4-6 White fabric layout.

3. Using the water-soluble pen, transfer a letter design from the Circus Alphabet, centering it in one white fabric square. Embroider the letters one at a time, using satin stitch for the main colors of the figures, a stem stitch for outlines when needed, and a chain stitch for the outline of the letter itself. (Follow the colors shown on the quilt in the color section or use colors of your own choosing.) In figures such as the elephant in the Q, where a lot of one color is used, work the satin stitch in sections so that the parts of the figure are defined. For example, the elephant's trunk is embroidered in one section, his ears in another, his head in another, and his legs in another.

4. When all the letters and the 2 stars have been embroidered, cut the white fabric squares apart. Use a pressing cloth and steam iron to block the letters.

5. Machine- or hand-stitch the letter squares and yellow squares together, making a $\frac{1}{2}''$ seam. First sew the squares together in rows. Press all seams. Then sew the rows together one row at a time, matching the corners. Press all seams using a pressing cloth.

6. Sew the two 52″-x-30″ yellow fabric pieces together, making a $\frac{1}{2}''$ seam along the 52″ side. Press the seam. This will make a 52″ x 59″ rectangle for the quilt backing.

7. Press the batting with a cool iron and pressing cloth to remove any large folds. Lay the batting between the yellow backing and the embroidered front, wrong sides against the batting. Pin. Hand baste the three sections together across the middle, lengthwise, diagonally, and around the edges, making sure all three pieces lie very flat and smooth.

8. Use a machine zigzag stitch or a small running stitch if sewing by hand to sew over each seam through all thicknesses of the quilt. Place pins along each seam before you sew to further stabilize the three sections of the quilt and remove the pins as you sew. Remove the basting. Press the quilt lightly using a pressing cloth. Trim the quilt backing and batting so that it is even with the quilt front.

9. Prepare all the edgings in the following manner. Turn under $\frac{1}{4}''$ along one long side of all edgings and press. Fold this turned-under edge toward the other long edge, wrong sides together, so that $\frac{1}{2}''$ of the unfolded edge extends beyond the folded edge. Press.

10. Pin the unfolded edge of a 56″ edging to the front side of the top of the quilt, right sides together, so that the ends of the edging extend equally. Sew by machine or by hand with a small running stitch, making a $\frac{1}{2}''$ seam. Press the seam. Sew the second 56″ edging to the bottom of the quilt in this manner. Press the seam.

11. Pin the unfolded edge of a 64″ edging to the front right hand side of the quilt, right sides together, so that the ends of the edging extend equally. (Note: Unfold the top and bottom edgings except for the $\frac{1}{4}''$ fold and pin the side edging to these as well as to the quilt.) Sew by machine or by hand using a small running stitch, making a $\frac{1}{2}''$ seam. Press the seam. Sew the second 64″ edging to the left hand side of the quilt, right sides together, in this manner. Press.

12. Trim off any excess edging at the corners. Fold the top edging to the back of the quilt along the previously pressed fold and pin. Press the edging at the corners. Sew the edging to the back of the quilt by hand using an invisible stitch. Finish the bottom and side edgings in this manner.

Special Ideas for Giving

Besides being warm and cozy, this quilt will help a lucky child learn his ABCs as well as introduce him to the wild and wonderful characters of the circus world. You may want to make up a few short stories about some of these characters. These stories could be told at bedtime, with the child and you wrapped up together in the ABC quilt. The child may want to make up some stories of his own about his new found friends, too! This quilt could be accompanied by a circus story book or coloring book to pique the child's interest.

SAMPLE STORY: The Pink Elephant

Once upon a time, there was a pink elephant who lived on a very special quilt, surrounded by his many circus friends. The pink elephant was very happy because he had just come to live with (child's name), and he knew that (child's name) would take very good care of him. But Mr. Pink Elephant had a problem! He couldn't eat anything but pink peanuts, and we all know that pink peanuts are very hard to find! Mr. Pink Elephant was getting thin and knew that something had to be done. He decided he would ask all of his circus friends if they knew where to find a pink peanut plant. (Have the child take an active part in talking to each animal and character. Between the two of you a solution to Mr. Elephant's problem can be found and the story completed.) And so Mr. Pink Elephant lived happily ever after in the Circus Quilt at (child's name) house because (name of circus character) had helped him find enough pink peanuts to last forever!

« Bunny Puppet »

½ yd 60"-wide white felt
2 9"-×-12" squares bright pink felt
2 ¾" wiggle eyes
Poly stuffing
4"-×-6" piece interfacing

1 2" white pom-pom
2 10" lengths white cotton-covered 30
  gauge wire
Craft glue

1. To make the arms and legs, cut out the pieces from white felt, pin the appropriate pieces together and stitch, using a ¼" seam. Trim the seam, turn right side out, and press. Stuff the arms and set aside. Stuff the feet up to the ankle and topstitch on the line indicated. Stuff the legs and set aside.

2. To make the ears, fold a 10" length of cotton-covered wire in half. Glue it to the center of one white ear, with the wire ends even with the bottom edge of the ear. Glue the pink inner ear over the white ear, centering it and having the bottom edges even. Fold the ear together at the bottom so that the pink felt is hidden. Now fold the excess white felt back. Baste ¼" from the bottom edge. Make a second ear in this manner. Set aside.

Fig. 4-7 Bunny puppet.

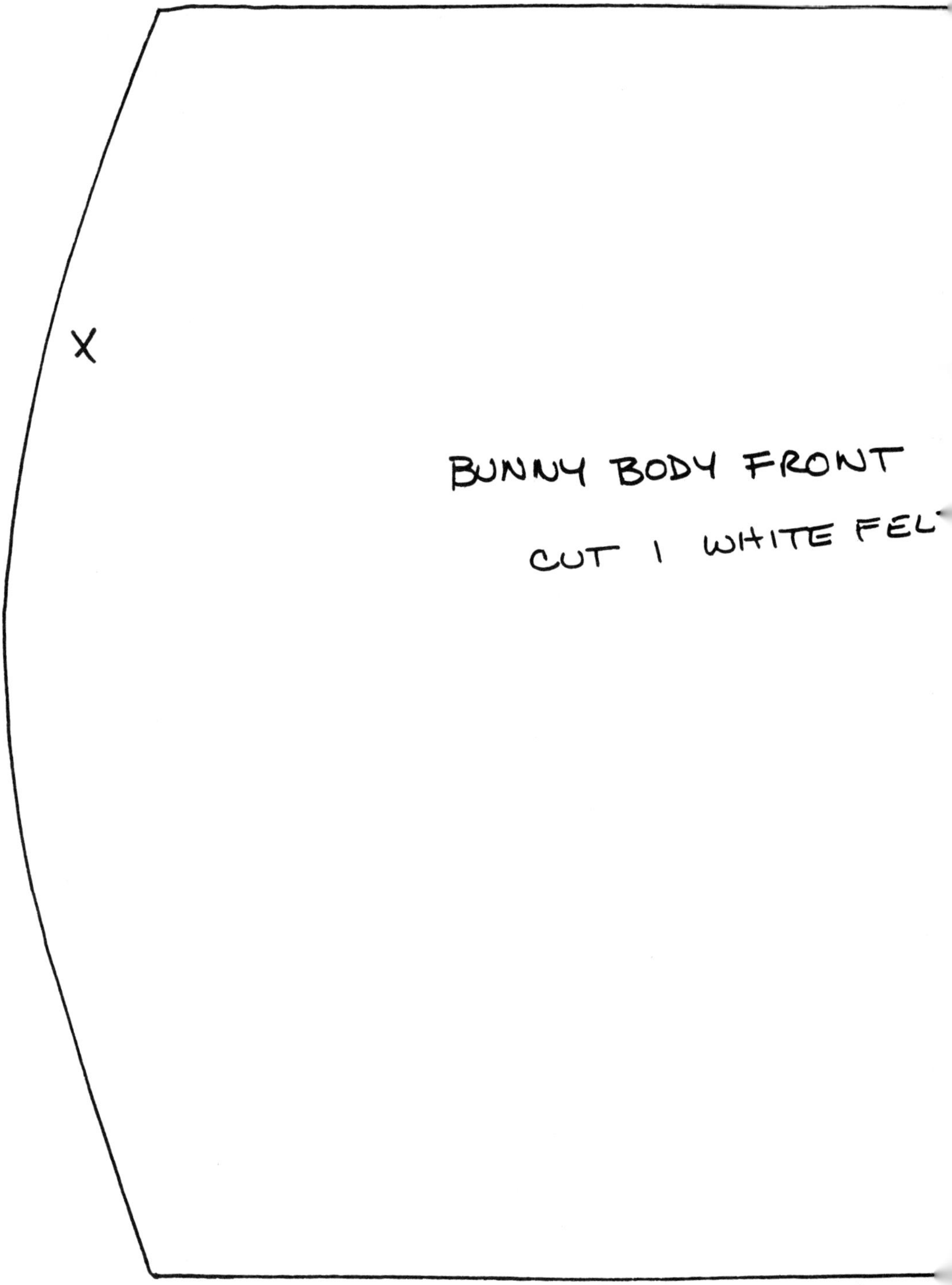

X

BUNNY BODY FRONT

CUT 1 WHITE FELT

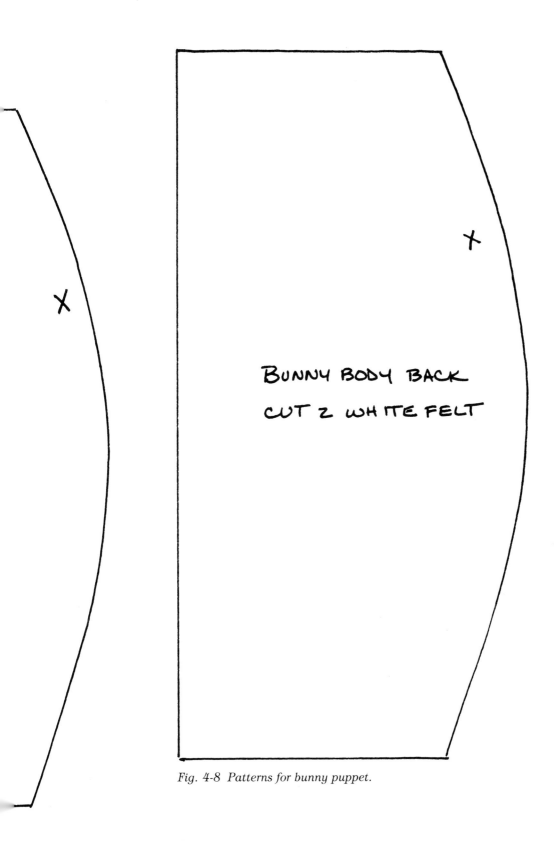

BUNNY BODY BACK
CUT 2 WHITE FELT

Fig. 4-8 Patterns for bunny puppet.

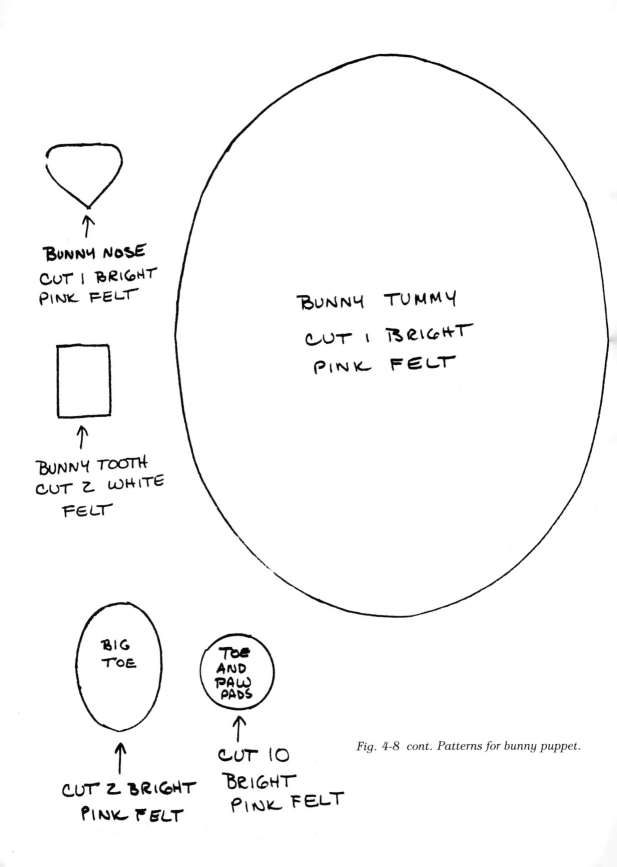

BUNNY NOSE
CUT 1 BRIGHT
PINK FELT

BUNNY TOOTH
CUT 2 WHITE
FELT

BUNNY TUMMY
CUT 1 BRIGHT
PINK FELT

BIG TOE

TOE AND PAW PADS

CUT 2 BRIGHT
PINK FELT

CUT 10
BRIGHT
PINK FELT

Fig. 4-8 cont. Patterns for bunny puppet.

BUNNY MOUTH

CUT 1 BRIGHT
PINK FELT AND
1 INTERFACING

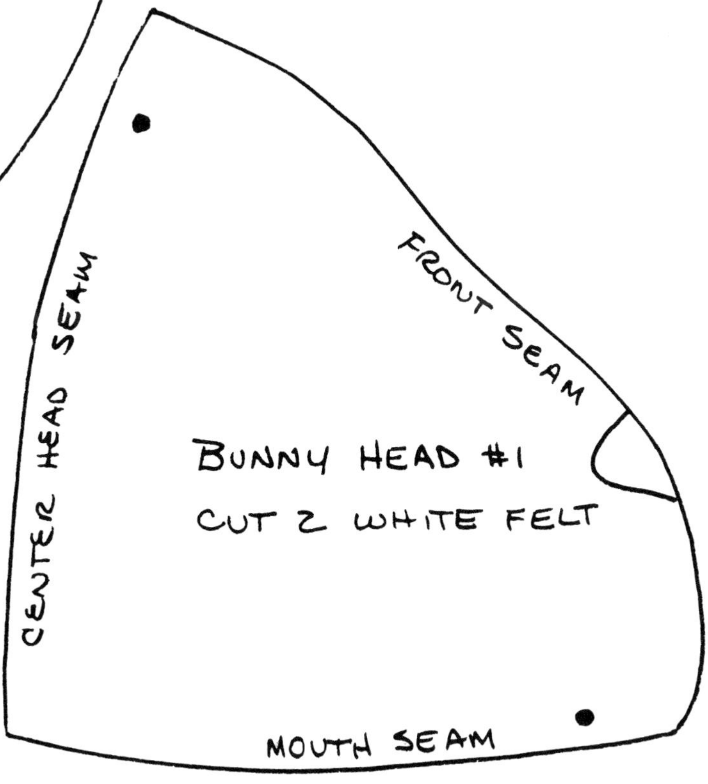

CENTER HEAD SEAM

FRONT SEAM

BUNNY HEAD #1

CUT 2 WHITE FELT

MOUTH SEAM

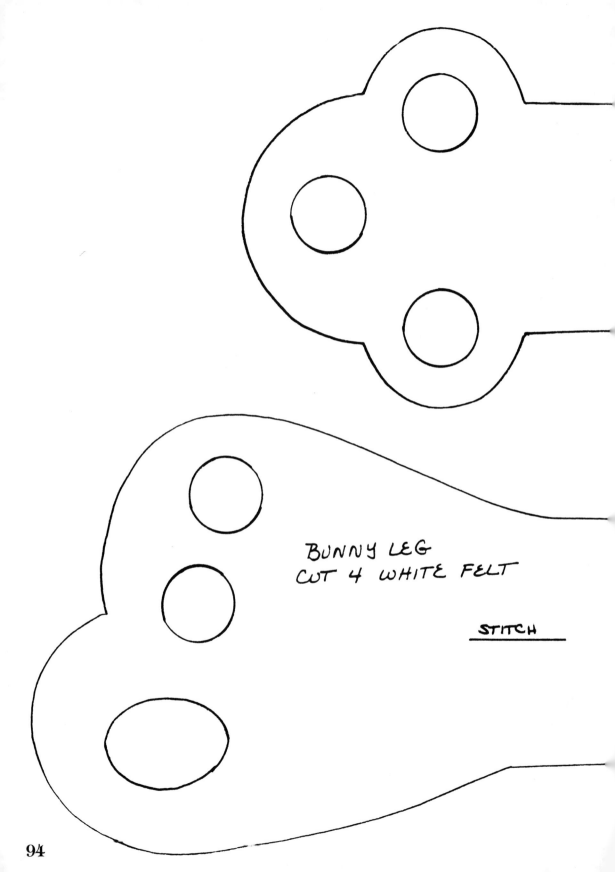

BUNNY LEG
CUT 4 WHITE FELT

STITCH

BUNNY ARM
CUT 4 WHITE FELT

Fig. 4-8 cont. Patterns for bunny puppet.

BUNNY LEG, cont.
CUT 4 WHITE FELT

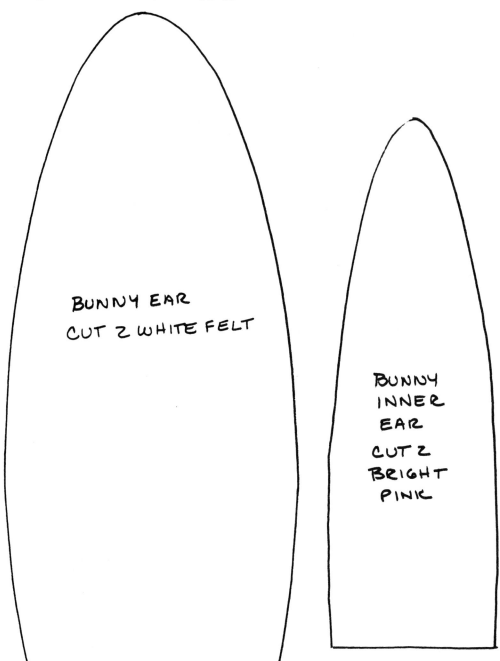

Fig. 4-8 cont. Patterns for bunny puppet.

BUNNY EAR
CUT 2 WHITE FELT

BUNNY
INNER
EAR
CUT 2
BRIGHT
PINK

+

CENTER HEAD SEAM

MOUTH SEAM

BACK SEAM

BUNNY HEAD #2
CUT 2 WHITE FELT

FRONT SEAM

NECK SEAM

3. Sew the front seam of bunny head #1, trim and press. Sew the front seam of bunny head #2, trim and press. Pin the bunny ears side by side into the back seam of bunny head #2 at the X. Stitch twice. Trim and press. Sew bunny head #1 to bunny head #2 at the center head seam. Trim and press. Tack the ears forward to the dots on bunny head #1.

4. To make the mouth, baste the white felt teeth to the center of the top of the bunny head mouth opening at the dots. Baste the interfacing to the pink felt mouth $\frac{1}{8}''$ away from the edge. Turn the head inside out. Pin the mouth to the head, right sides together, and stitch, using a $\frac{1}{4}''$ seam. Trim, turn and press. Set the head aside.

5. To make the body, stitch the back seam $\frac{1}{2}''$ down from the top and 2'' up from the bottom. Press the seam and topstitch the opening for strength. Pin the bunny front to the bunny back, pinning the stuffed arms into the side seams at the Xs and stitch. Trim the seam and press.

6. To assemble, pin the stuffed bunny legs onto the bottom of the body, right sides together, with the feet facing front and the large toes in the middle. Stitch, trim and press. Pin the head to the neck of the body, right sides together. Stitch, trim and press.

7. Glue on the nose, eyes, tail, tummy and paw pads as indicated. Feed carrots once a day!

Special Ideas for Giving

his silly bunny needs something to fill him up! Take a trip to the local dimestore and walk through the "penny" toy section. You'll find many little objects there, such as crayons, blowing bubbles, modeling clay, and an old-fashioned "jacks" game. Wrap these surprises in colorful tissue paper and place them carefully inside the rabbit. Instead of wrapping him up in a box, why not present him in a fashion that reflects his personality? Find a big Easter basket, fill it with Easter grass or crinkled tissue paper, add a bow and place Mr. Bunny in the center. He's a cute present for any occasion, but especially perfect for Easter!

« Ballerina Puppet »

⅓ yd 60"-wide light pink felt
2 9"-×-12" squares white felt
6"-×-4" remnant bright pink felt
3 yd ⅝"-wide pink satin picot-edge
   ribbon
Poly stuffing

Black sequins
Craft glue
2½"-×-¾" oval wiggle eyes
Yellow worsted weight yarn
12"-×-36" piece pink tulle

    1. To make the arms, pin two felt arm pieces together and stitch using a ¼" seam. Trim the seam, turn right side out, press and stuff. Set aside.

    2. To make the legs, sew the slippers to the feet, overlapping the slipper tops ¼" onto the feet and topstitching. Pin two leg pieces right sides together, stitch, trim the seam, and turn right side out. Press and stuff. Glue an 18" length of ribbon to each side of the foot at the X. Wrap around the leg as shown and tie in a bow. Set aside.

    3. To make the head, stitch head #1 together along the front seam. Trim the seam and press. Stitch head #2 together along the back and front seams,

Fig. 4-9 Ballerina puppet.

Fig. 4-10 Ballerina pattern. Use size shown.

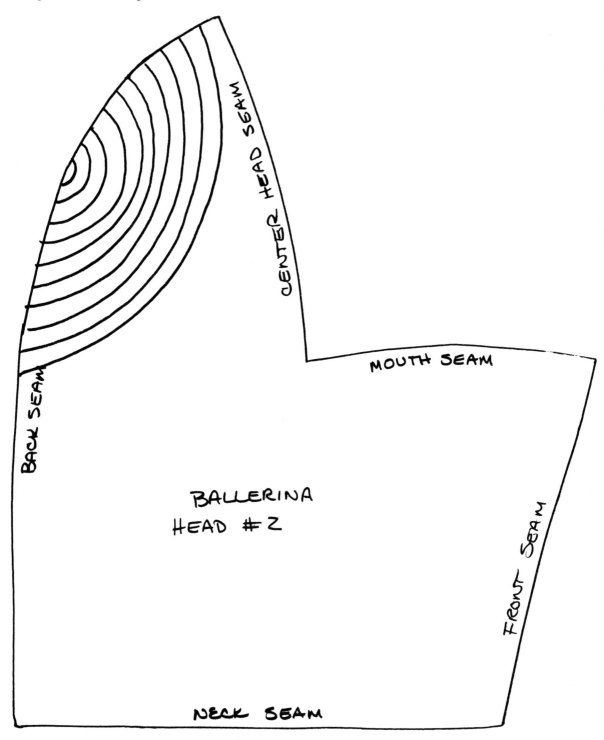

CENTER HEAD SEAM

MOUTH SEAM

BACK SEAM

BALLERINA
HEAD #2

FRONT SEAM

NECK SEAM

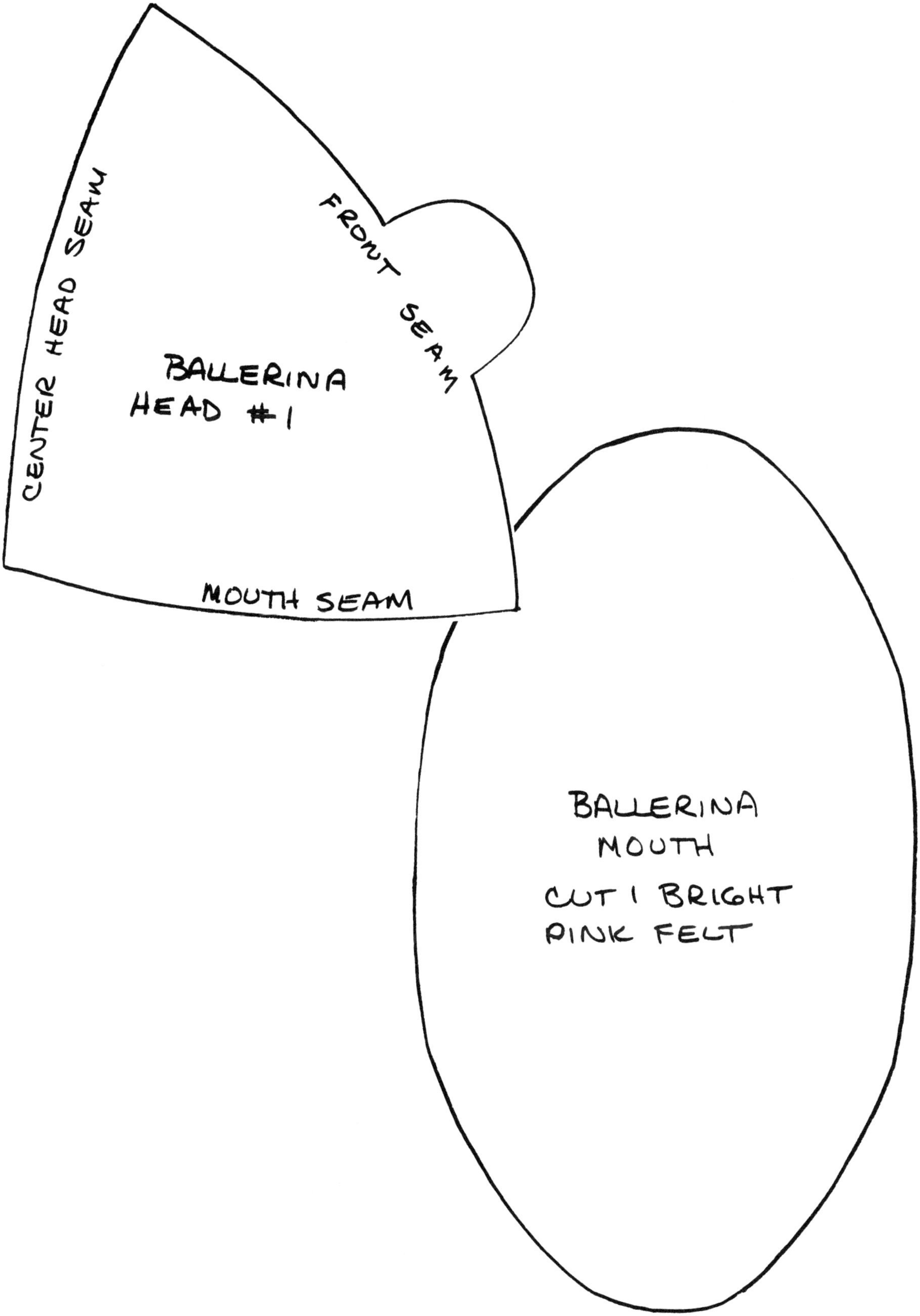

CENTER HEAD SEAM

FRONT SEAM

BALLERINA
HEAD #1

MOUTH SEAM

BALLERINA
MOUTH

CUT 1 BRIGHT
PINK FELT

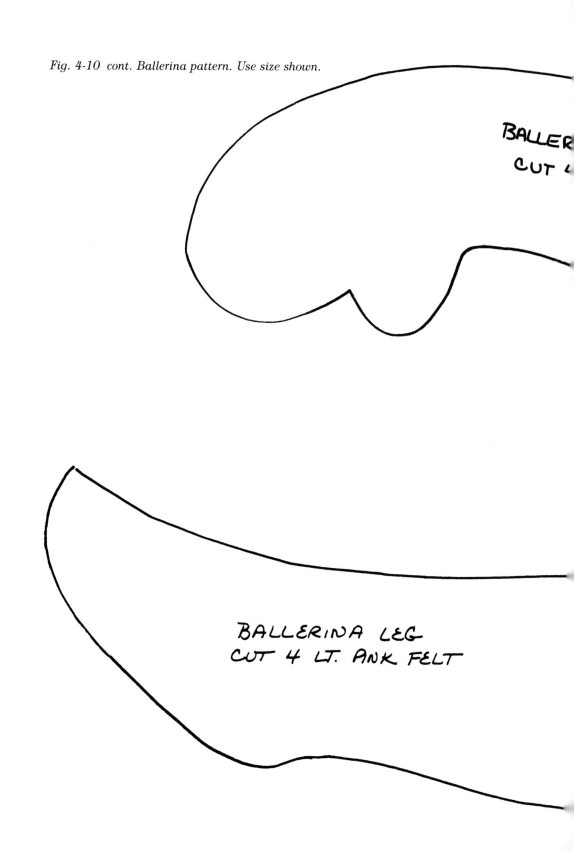

Fig. 4-10 cont. Ballerina pattern. Use size shown.

BALLER

CUT

BALLERINA LEG
CUT 4 LT. PINK FELT

A ARM
LT. PINK FELT

BALLERINA
SLIPPER
CUT 4 WHITE FELT

BALLERINA LEG
CUT 4 LT. PINK FELT

103

BALLERINA BODY FRONT
CUT 1 LT. PINK FELT

X   X

BALLERINA BODICE
FRONT
CUT 1 WHITE FELT

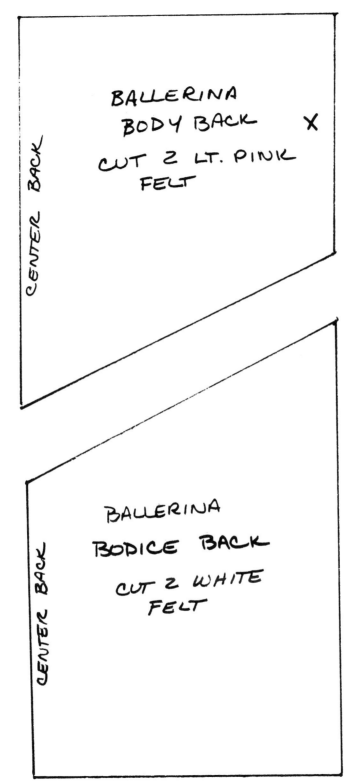

Fig. 4-10 cont. Ballerina patterns. Use size shown.

trim and press. Stitch heads #1 and #2 together at the center head seam. Trim and press. Pin the pink mouth to the mouth opening with right sides together. Stitch, trim and turn right side out. Topstitch around the mouth close to the edge. Glue on the eyes.

4. To make the hair, start at the crown of the head and glue on the yarn in a circular fashion, following the lines shown on the pattern piece, head #2. Make the braid by cutting 21 1-yd lengths of yarn. Braid loosely, using 7 strands for each section. Glue the braid to the head at the edge of the glued-on yarn, with the braid ends at the back of the head. Cut off any excess braid and tie the braid ends securely together. Make a bow with an 18″ length of ribbon and glue to the braid at this point.

5. To make the body, overlap the white felt bodice front onto the pink body front ¼″ and topstitch. Overlap the white felt bodice backs onto the pink felt body backs ¼″ and topstitch. Stitch the two back sections together ¾″ down from the top and ¾″ up from the bottom. Press under ¼″ along the opening and topstitch.

6. To assemble, pin the arms to the sides at the Xs, with the hands curving in and right sides together. Stitch the side seams. Trim and press. Pin the legs to the body bottom, with right sides together and the toes pointing out. Stitch, trim, turn right side out, and press. Pin the head to the body with the right sides together. Stitch, trim, turn right side out, and press.

7. To make the tutu, fold the tulle in half so that it measures 6″ x 1 yd. Run two rows of gathering stitches along this fold. Adjust the gathers to fit the waistline. Pin along the waistline and baste. Stitch ribbon over the basting, turning under ½″ at each end. Glue sequins over the stitching line.

Special Ideas for Giving

his ballerina puppet looks a little sad when she's all empty inside, so stuff her with something happy and delicious, such as a batch of the child's favorite cookies. Wrap them carefully to avoid any grease spots, before slipping them into the puppet. Then wrap our Miss Ballerina in something worthy of her sophistication, such as an old-fashioned round hat box. Set her gently into layers of crinkled colorful tissue paper and top with a big satin bow. The delighted child may want to keep this hat box as Miss Ballerina's permanent home.

« Felt Animal Sachets »

PIG

9"- × -12" square light pink felt
Pink and black #5 DMC embroidery
  thread
Small amount bright pink felt

Poly stuffing
Potpourri or concentrated liquid scent
Craft glue
Disappearing ink pen

1. Fold the light pink felt square in half so that the pig pattern fits onto it. Cut along the fold. Trace the pig pattern onto the felt using the disappearing ink pen. Pin the felt pieces together. Stitch along the line, leaving open between the dots. Trim close to the stitching. Stuff with poly stuffing and some pot-pourri, or use liquid scent instead of potpourri. Stitch the opening closed.

2. Cut out a small semicircle of bright pink felt for the snout. Glue onto the face as shown. Using French knots and backstitch, embroider the eye, nostril, and mouth. To make the tail, sew three 8" lengths of pink embroidery

Fig. 4-11 Felt animal sachets.

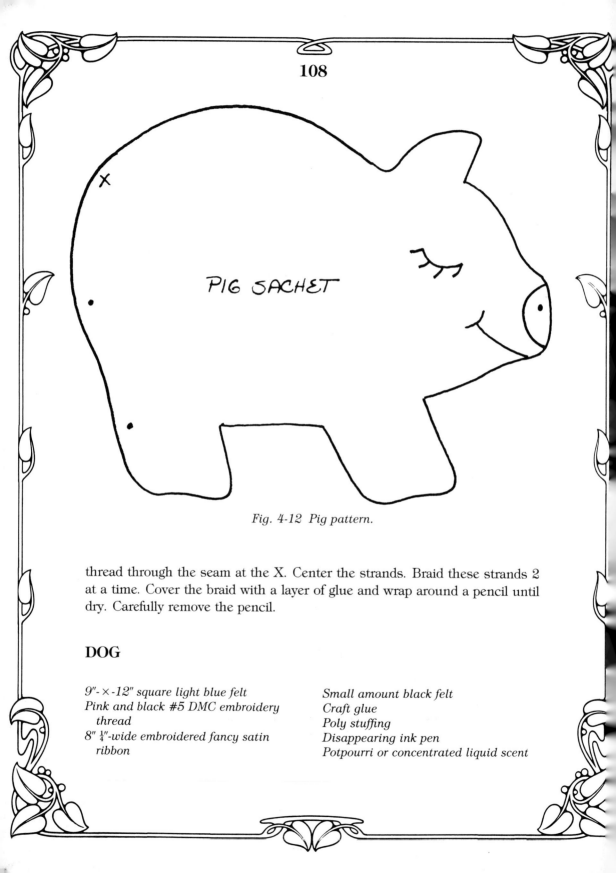

Fig. 4-12 Pig pattern.

thread through the seam at the X. Center the strands. Braid these strands 2 at a time. Cover the braid with a layer of glue and wrap around a pencil until dry. Carefully remove the pencil.

DOG

9"-×-12" square light blue felt
Pink and black #5 DMC embroidery
   thread
8" ¼"-wide embroidered fancy satin
   ribbon

Small amount black felt
Craft glue
Poly stuffing
Disappearing ink pen
Potpourri or concentrated liquid scent

Fig. 4-13 Dog pattern.

1. Assemble as you did the pig. Cut out eye and nose shapes from the black felt and glue onto the face. Embroider the mouth and freckles using backstitch and French knots. Stitch through all thicknesses along the lines indicated for extra shape. Make a bow and glue on at the neck.

CAT

9"- × -12" square light purple felt
Small amount light pink and black felt
8" $\frac{1}{4}$"-wide embroidered fancy satin
  ribbon
Pink and black #5 DMC embroidery
  thread

Poly stuffing
Potpourri or concentrated liquid scent
Disappearing ink pen

Fig. 4-14 Cat pattern.

1. Assemble as you did the pig and dog. Cut out nose, ear and eye shapes from the appropriate color felt and glue onto the face. Using a backstitch, embroider on the mouth and whiskers. Sew through all thicknesses along the lines indicated for extra shape. Make a bow and glue on at the neck.

Special Ideas for Giving

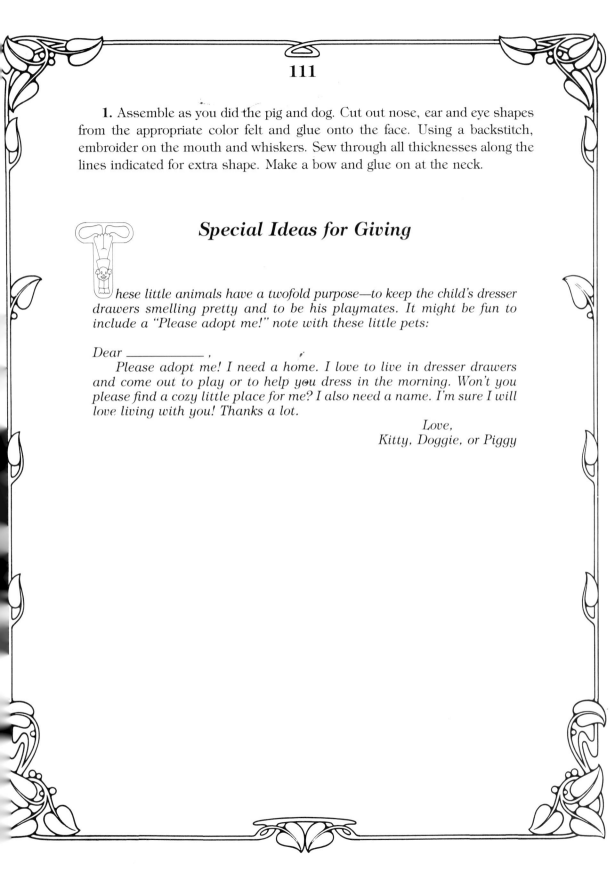

hese little animals have a twofold purpose—to keep the child's dresser drawers smelling pretty and to be his playmates. It might be fun to include a "Please adopt me!" note with these little pets:

Dear _____ ,
Please adopt me! I need a home. I love to live in dresser drawers and come out to play or to help you dress in the morning. Won't you please find a cozy little place for me? I also need a name. I'm sure I will love living with you! Thanks a lot.

Love,
Kitty, Doggie, or Piggy

« Heart Mobile »

4 yd ⅜"-wide yellow grosgrain ribbon
9" diameter clear plastic ring
2" diameter plastic ring
Fish line
Craft glue

Poly stuffing
Scallop shears (or pinking shears)
9" × 12" squares of felt: red, orange,
   yellow, green, blue, and purple
Thread to match felt

1. Cut out 4 hearts of each color felt. To cut, first pin the heart pattern to the felt and cut around the heart with the scallop shears, cutting through 2 thicknesses at once.

2. Using the matching thread, stitch ¼" in from the edge of the scallop, leaving open between the dots. Stuff and stitch the opening closed. Make 2 hearts of each color.

3. Measure three 1 yd lengths of ribbon. Attach each of these to the large ring at equidistant points, by wrapping the end around the ring and sewing the ribbon to itself. Secure the ribbon to the ring with a dot of glue.

Fig. 4-15 Heart mobile.

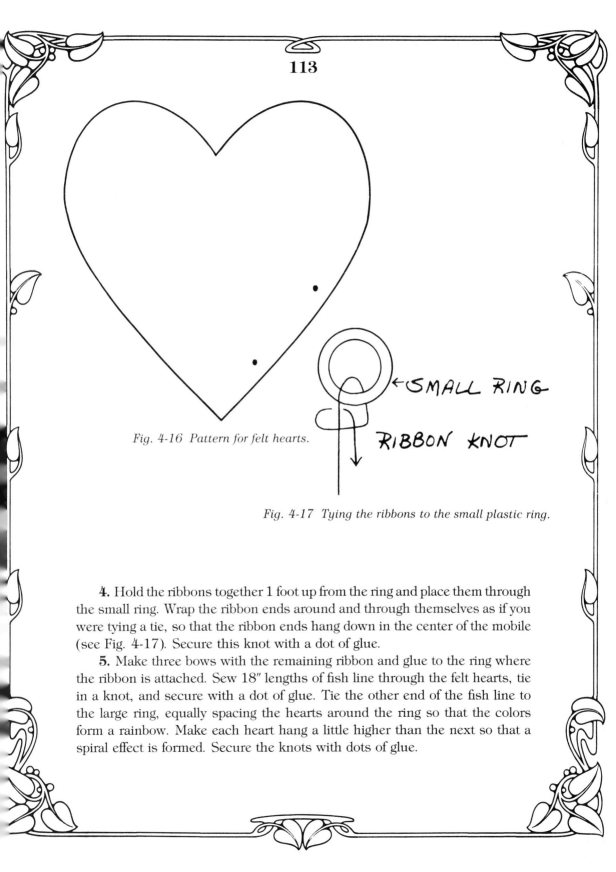

Fig. 4-16 Pattern for felt hearts.

←SMALL RING

RIBBON KNOT

Fig. 4-17 Tying the ribbons to the small plastic ring.

4. Hold the ribbons together 1 foot up from the ring and place them through the small ring. Wrap the ribbon ends around and through themselves as if you were tying a tie, so that the ribbon ends hang down in the center of the mobile (see Fig. 4-17). Secure this knot with a dot of glue.

5. Make three bows with the remaining ribbon and glue to the ring where the ribbon is attached. Sew 18″ lengths of fish line through the felt hearts, tie in a knot, and secure with a dot of glue. Tie the other end of the fish line to the large ring, equally spacing the hearts around the ring so that the colors form a rainbow. Make each heart hang a little higher than the next so that a spiral effect is formed. Secure the knots with dots of glue.

Special Ideas for Giving

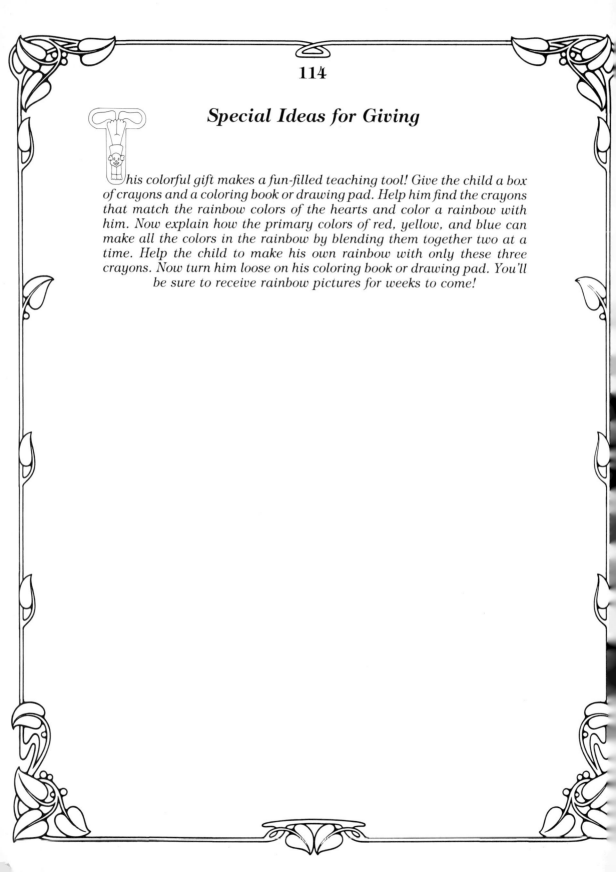

This colorful gift makes a fun-filled teaching tool! Give the child a box of crayons and a coloring book or drawing pad. Help him find the crayons that match the rainbow colors of the hearts and color a rainbow with him. Now explain how the primary colors of red, yellow, and blue can make all the colors in the rainbow by blending them together two at a time. Help the child to make his own rainbow with only these three crayons. Now turn him loose on his coloring book or drawing pad. You'll be sure to receive rainbow pictures for weeks to come!

5

SPECIAL TECHNIQUES

« Perfect Bows »

How many times have you wished you could snap your fingers and instantly have a perfect bow to decorate a special gift? And how many times have you had to give up and tape a purchased paper ribbon bow onto the present? If your answer is a grumbly "Don't Ask!", then this bow-making section is for you.

With a yard or two of craft ribbon, a ruler, and a bit of 30-gauge wire you will now be able to make a perfect bow in any size you want. Follow the Ribbon Chart to determine how much ribbon your bow will use. The narrower the ribbon, the smaller your finished bow will be.

RIBBON CHART

Ribbon No.	Ribbon Width	Yardage	Fold Over	Distance Between Loops
100	4"	$3\frac{1}{2}$	10"	15"
40	$2\frac{5}{8}$"	3	8"	12"
16	$1\frac{7}{8}$"	$2\frac{1}{2}$	7"	10"
9	$1\frac{3}{8}$"	$1\frac{1}{2}$	4"	6"
5	$\frac{7}{8}$"	$1\frac{1}{4}$	3"	5"
3	$\frac{5}{8}$"	1	$2\frac{1}{2}$"	4"

Now follow these steps:

1. Hold the ribbon with the wrong side of the ribbon facing you. Fold over the proper amount of ribbon (see chart) to form a loop on the right end. See Fig. 5-1.

2. Fold the other end of the ribbon toward you, forming a loop on the left side. Measure the distance between the loops according to the Ribbon Chart. See Fig. 5-2.

3. Continue making loops by wrapping the ribbon around the original loops until there are three loops on each end. Measure in from the left loops the same amount you originally folded over, and cut off the ribbon at this point. See Fig. 5-3.

4. Fold the looped ribbon in half and cut through all thicknesses in a V shape on each side of the fold. Leave enough ribbon in the center to form a pleat. See Fig. 5-4.

5. Depending on the width of ribbon, cut a 6- to 10-inch piece of 30 gauge wrapping wire. Fold the notched center section into a pleat and secure with a wrap and tight twist of the wire. Separate the loops of the bow, one at a time, pulling the innermost loops on each side to the top and the next layer of inside loops to the bottom. Fluff the loops to make a full bow. See Fig. 5-5.

6. Fold the remaining ribbon in half, but *Do not crease the fold.* Gather 1 to 3 inches from the folded end. Secure this gather with another piece of 30 gauge wire. Fluff the gathered section to form the "knot" of the bow. Pull the ribbon ends down to form the streamers. Cut the ribbon ends in a V shape. See Fig. 5-6.

7. Attach the knot and streamers to the bow by slipping one end of the remaining wire between the top loops and the other end between the bottom loops. See Fig. 5-7. Twist the wire ends together in the back to secure. The excess wire may be used to attach your bow to your project or package.

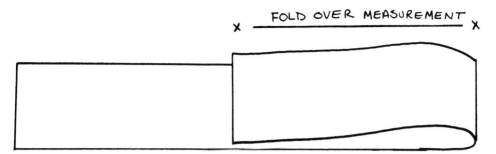

Fig. 5-1 Bow step 1.

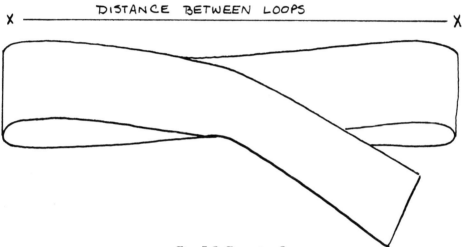

Fig. 5-2 Bow step 2.

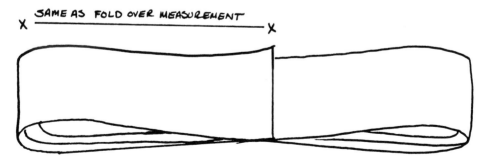

Fig. 5-3 Bow step 3.

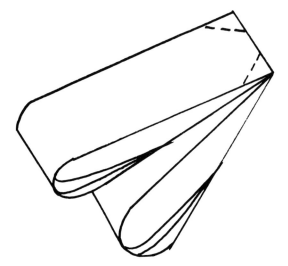

Fig. 5-4 Bow step 4.

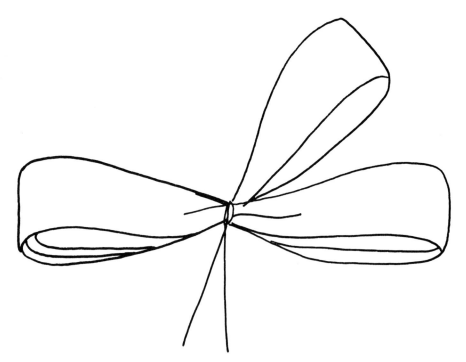

Fig. 5-5 Bow step 5.

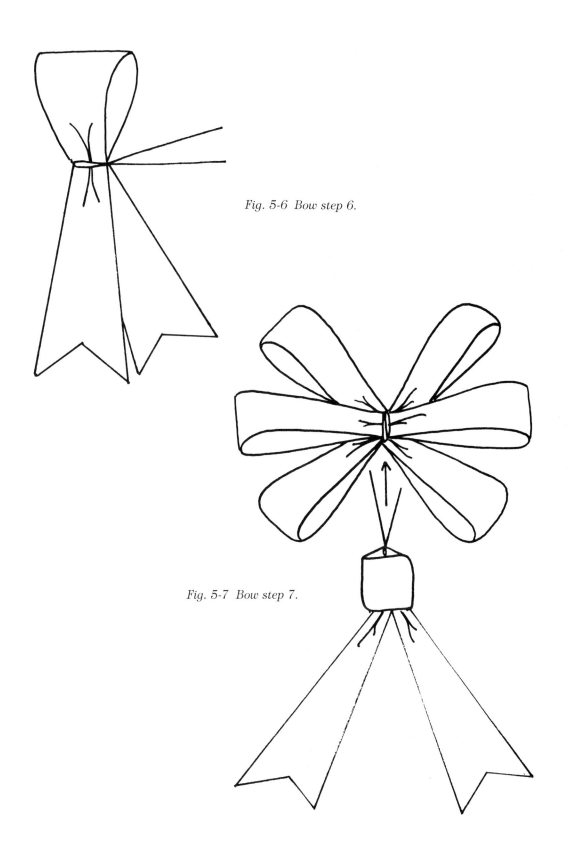

Fig. 5-6 Bow step 6.

Fig. 5-7 Bow step 7.

« Potpourri »

Potpourri is wonderful to have around the house, because it's like having a bit of fragrant summertime always with you! When you give a friend a gift of potpourri, it is a gift of summer sunshine. If you love flowers and gardening, you will love making potpourri.

CUTTING AND DRYING

First you must gather the flowers. Cut them in the afternoon when all the dew has dried from them, and always choose the flowers that are in the best condition. Dropped petals from cut flowers in the house are fine to use as long as they are unblemished. Avoid thick fleshy flowers, and with flowers that have thick hard centers, use only the petals.

Choose an airy, dark place in which to dry your flowers. A damp place may cause the flowers to rot, too much warmth will dry out the fragrant oils, and too much light will fade the colors. A dry closet, dry corner of a basement, or even underneath your bed will suffice. Spread the leaves and petals thinly on a piece of paper or muslin fabric. Turn the petals regularly. They will be ready for potpourri when they are crisply dry and rustle when shaken.

Rosebuds or other small flowers you wish to remain intact should be dried in silica gel to avoid any possibility of rotting. Silica gel resembles a fine dry sand and acts as a sponge, absorbing water equal to 40 times its weight. You can buy it at a florist or craft shop. Just immerse the flowers in the sand and wait several days. Test the flower by pressing it gently between your thumb and forefinger. If the bud feels hard instead of resilient, it is ready for your potpourri.

After making your potpourri, allow it to "mix" for several weeks, tossing it gently with your hand occasionally to mingle the scents. You may want to add little surprises to it from time to time to reawaken its aroma, such as mint leaves, a pinch of spice, a piece of ginger root or dried orange peel, a clove, or a drop of vanilla.

FLOWERS, HERBS, AND SPICES

Use a variety of colors and scents together, adapting these recipes according to what is available from your garden or florist. Have fun experimenting to achieve your own distinctive blend. Remember, this is your creation!

The following flowers and leaves are especially good for retaining a pretty scent: Flowers of roses, lavender, violets, jasmine, orange blossom, lilac, peony, honeysuckle, and heliotrope; leaves of geranium, lemon verbena, bay, box, sweet myrtle, and eucalyptus.

The following flowers are expecially good for retaining their color: larkspur, cornflower, marigold, nasturtium, pansies, hydrangea, forget-me-not, zinnias, and all "daisy-shaped" flowers.

Herbs to use: basil, marjoram, rosemary, thyme, sage, tarragon, dill, mint, spearmint, peppermint, sweet wormwood, woodruff, and southernwood.

Fixatives to use: orris root, vetiver, gum benzoin, calamus, tonquin bean, myrrh, frankincense, and oakmoss. Note: The fixative will help to retard evaporation of natural oils, but its use is optional.

Spices to use: allspice, anise, cardamom, coriander, caraway, cinnamon, cloves, mace, and nutmeg.

Other ingredients to add interest: cedarwood or sandalwood chips; ginger root; lemon, lime, orange or tangerine peel (dried and crushed), vanilla pod, cinnamon stick, juniper berries, cloves and peppercorns.

Oils to use: Flowery Scent—rose, honeysuckle, jasmine, lilac. Fresh Scent—orange, lemon verbena. Herby Scent—thyme, rosemary, sage, lavender. Woody Scent—cedarwood, sandalwood. Exotic Scent—musk, vanilla. Note: These and many other oils can be found in craft stores.

TWO RECIPES

Here are two classic potpourri recipes you may wish to follow, but remember, have fun and experiment!

Recipe 1

1 quart rose petals
1 pint geranium leaves
½ pint lavender flowers
½ pint rosemary leaves
1 tablespoon marjoram
1 tablespoon crushed orris root
½ tablespoon cloves
½ tablespoon nutmeg
10 drops rose oil
6 drops lemon verbena oil
3 drops lavender oil

Recipe 2

1 quart rose petals
½ pint lavender flowers
1 tablespoon crushed orris root
1 teaspoon anise seed
1 tablespoon broken cloves and
  cinnamon stick
4 drops each of the following oils:
  jasmine, rose, geranium, rosemary

« Ribbon Roses »

The basic folded "package" rose is an all-time favorite with crafters. It is usually made out of ribbon, but it can also be made out of fabric cut on the bias to minimize unraveling. Organdy makes a lovely bloom, or use fabric that matches the piece you are embellishing. Both sides of the fabric or ribbon will show, since the rose is made by folding, so choose fabric or ribbon which is pretty on both sides!

The size of the rose you produce will be determined by the width of ribbon or fabric strip you use. A #40 ribbon, which is about $2\frac{5}{8}''$ wide, make a full-size rose. A #9 ribbon, which measures about $1\frac{3}{8}''$, makes a "sweetheart" size rose. A #3 ribbon, which measures about $\frac{5}{8}''$, makes a very petite miniature rose. With these three sizes of rose, you will be able to decorate just about any project you can dream up.

Follow the basic instructions to make any of these sizes of rose, using the amount of ribbon called for in the materials list for your project, or follow the Ribbon Rose Chart shown here.

RIBBON ROSE CHART

Ribbon No.	Ribbon Width	Length For 1 Rose
40	$2\frac{5}{8}''$	36"
9	$1\frac{3}{8}''$	15"
5	$\frac{7}{8}''$	12"
3	$\frac{5}{8}''$	8"

1. Fold one end of the ribbon toward you on a 90-degree angle, leaving a 1" tail. (Fig. 5-8.)

2. Roll the ribbon that has been folded from the right side to the left, stopping at the left edge of the folded ribbon. (Fig. 5-9.)

3. Secure this rolled section with a 9" piece of wrapping wire (30 gauge) where it meets the remaining ribbon. This forms the core of the rose. (Fig. 5-10.)

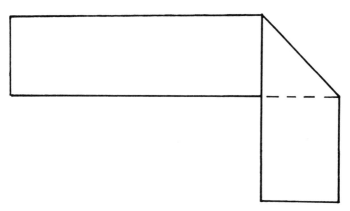

Fig. 5-8 Rose step 1.

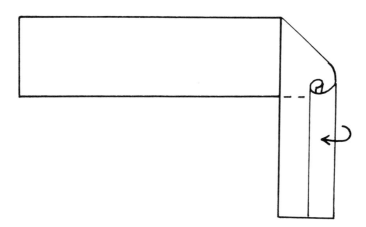

Fig. 5-9 Rose step 2.

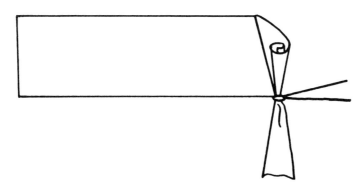

Fig. 5-10 Rose step 3.

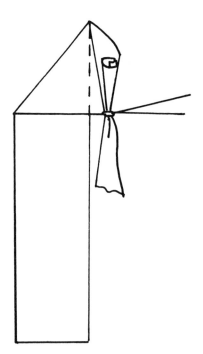

Fig. 5-11 Rose step 4.

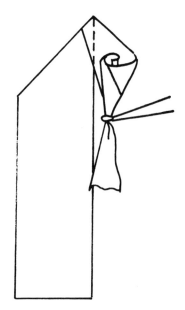

Fig. 5-12 Rose step 5.

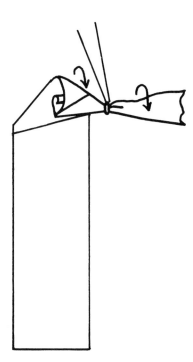

Fig. 5-13 Rose step 6.

Fig. 5-14 Rose step 7.

4. Fold the remaining ribbon away from yourself, bringing the ribbon parallel with the core. (Fig. 5-11.)

5. Pull the remaining ribbon up gently with your left hand, tightening it at the base of the rose and keeping it in place with your right index finger. Use your left thumb to push back on the top half of the ribbon so that the angle of fold remains as close to 90 degrees as possible. (Fig. 5-12.)

6. Turn the core of the rose to the left and fold the ribbon away from yourself at a point approxmately $\frac{1}{4}''$ in from the 90-degree fold. Bring the ribbon down parallel to the core as before, tightening it at the base. (Note: The rose must stay together because of the ribbon folds hugging the rolled center. When the rose is finished, these folds will look like a camera lens shutter, when the rose is viewed from the bottom. The tighter these folds are, the more secure the rose will be.) (Fig 5-13.)

7. Pull the ribbon up, turning the center of the rose and tightening by pushing the ribbon with your left thumb as before. Fold again as in step 6. Continue this process until all but 1″ of the ribbon is used. Catch the remaining ribbon with a wrap of the 30-gauge wire. (Fig. 5-14.)

8. Finish the rose by cutting off any excess wire ends and ribbon. Wrap tightly with floral tape if desired.

SPECIAL TIPS FOR SATIN RIBBON

Most of the ribbon used in craft projects has been sized to add body and prevent unraveling. Satin ribbon, however, is not sized and is soft and slippery. Follow these extra steps when making a rose out of satin ribbon to prevent the rose from popping apart.

1. Have a needle threaded and knotted and ready to use before you begin.

2. Instead of using wire to secure your rose, use the thread. Let the needle and thread hang down as you fold the ribbon to form the rose.

3. Finish the rose by wrapping and stitching with the needle and thread. Then pass the needle up through the center of the rose and back down again making a very small stitch. Do this twice to secure the center.

6

ALPHABET PATTERNS

This chapter contains patterns for two alphabets: the Circus ABC Counted Cross Stitch Names, and outlines for the Circus Alphabet Quilt. Simple block letters and numerals are helpful for many projects, and can be found on page 55.

GENERAL INSTRUCTIONS FOR COUNTED CROSS STITCH ABCs:

The designs are worked entirely in cross stitch, with outline details done in back stitch. Other details, such as whiskers and mouths, are done in long stitch. Each square on the graph equals one cross stitch over one block on the fabric. Work horizontal rows of cross stitch in two separate journeys—first the underside from left to right (Fig. 6-1a), then the top of the cross from right to left (Fig. 6-1b). Work any outline and long stitch details after all the cross stitches are completed. The use of an embroidery hoop or frame is suggested. The "count" Aida cloth you choose will determine the finished size of your work, so choose accordingly. Your finished piece may be lightly pressed with a steam iron from the wrong side.

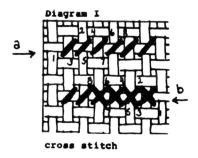

Fig. 6-1 Cross stitch.

Fig. 6-2 Color guide for counted cross stitch ABCs.

128

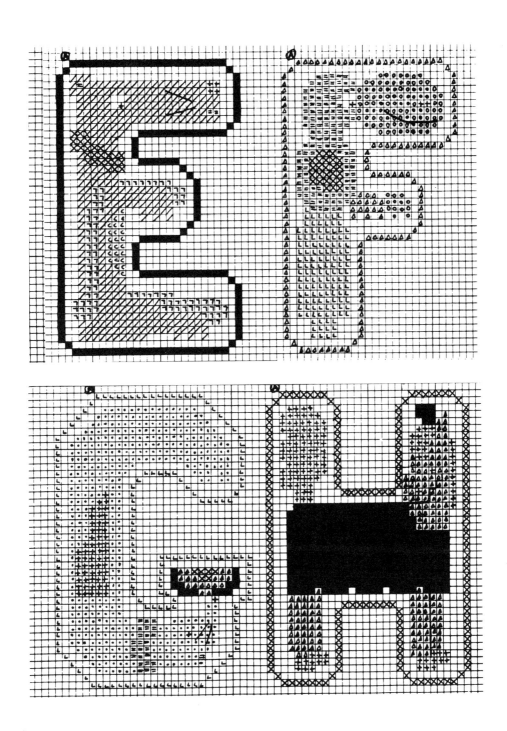

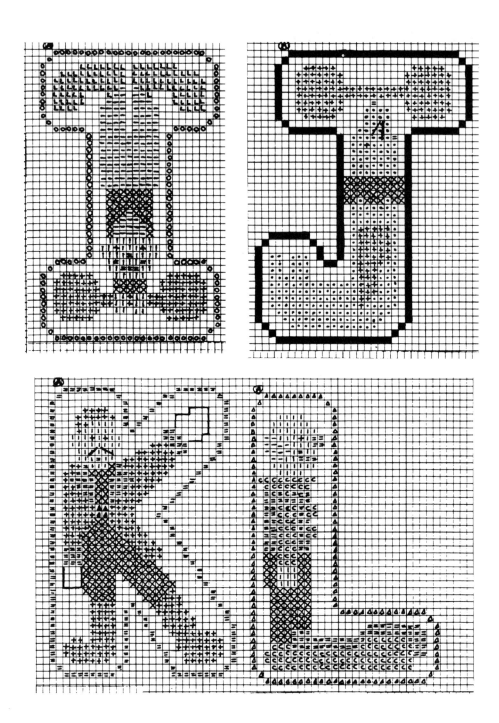

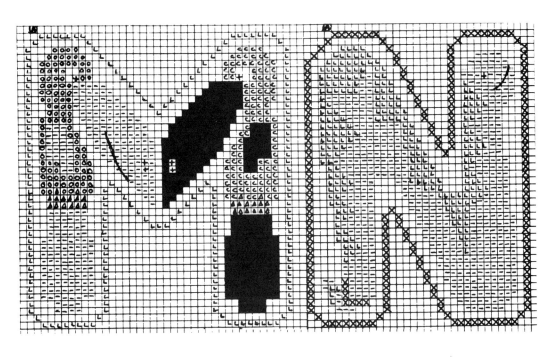

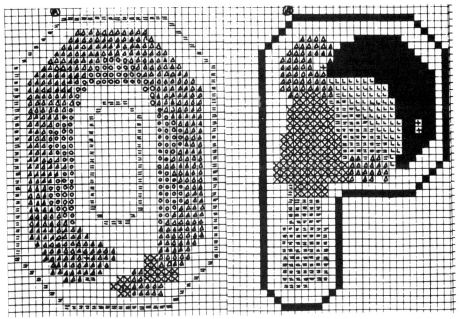

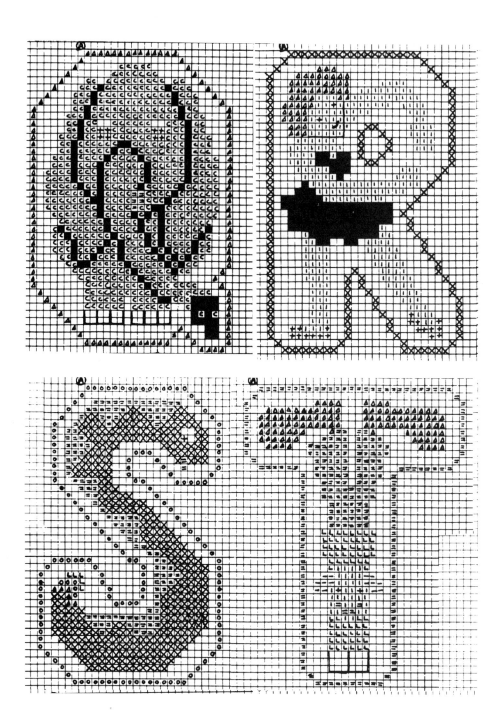

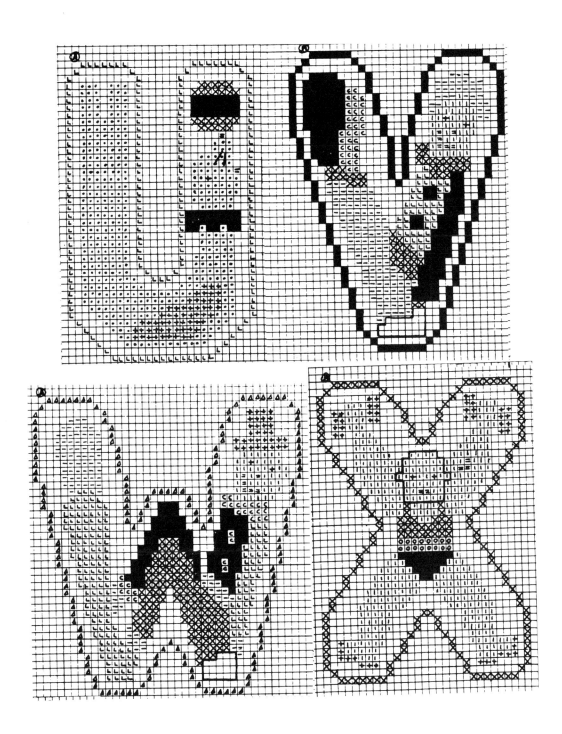

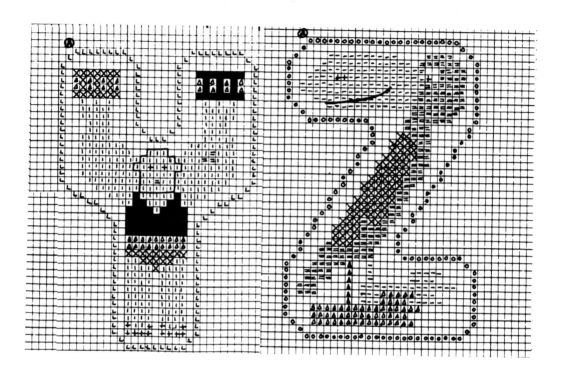

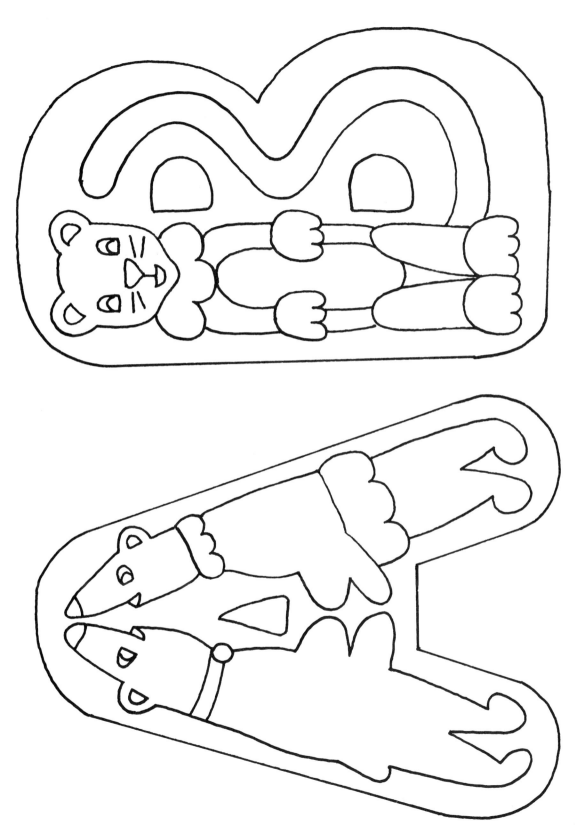

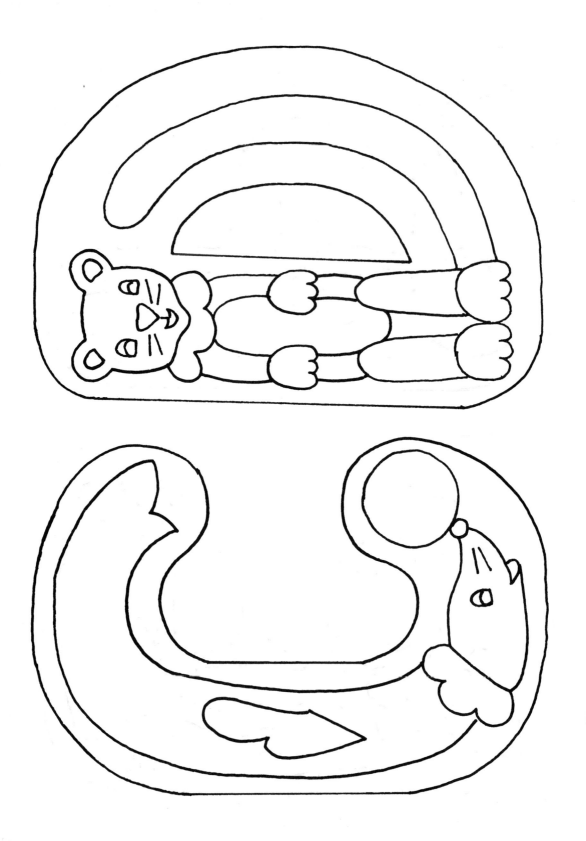

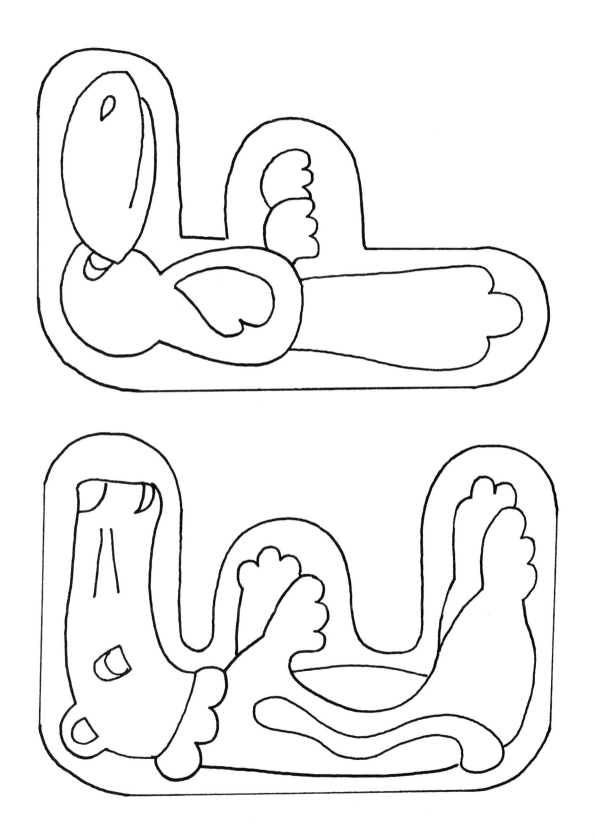

137

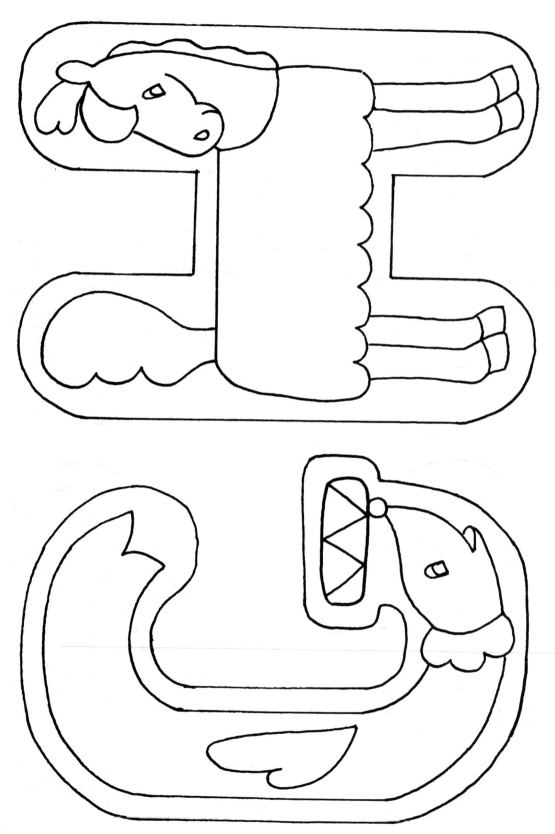

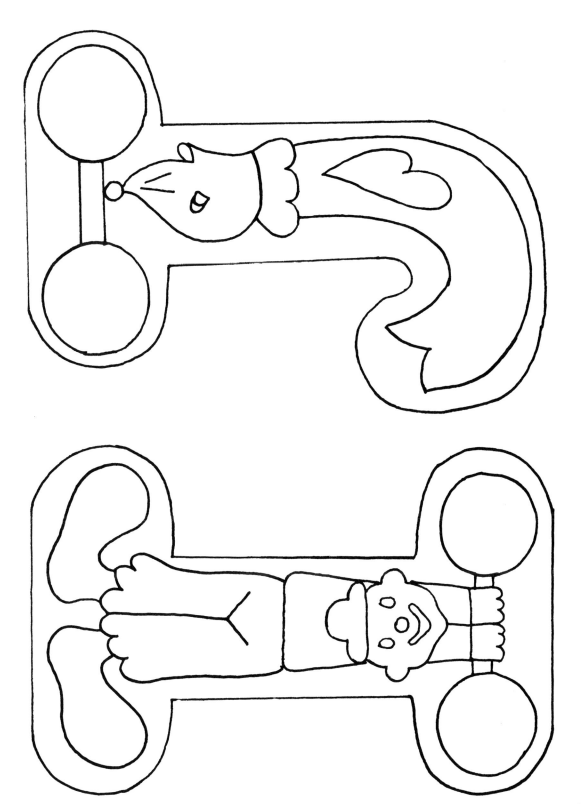

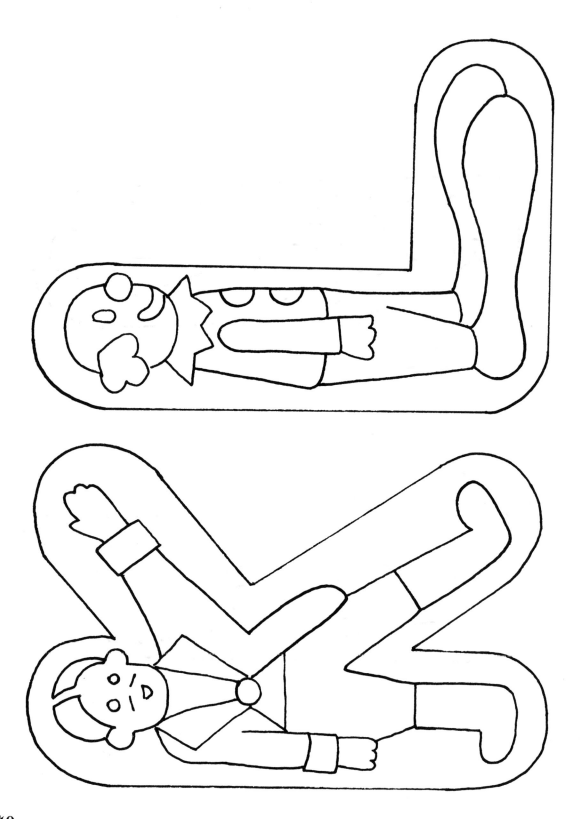

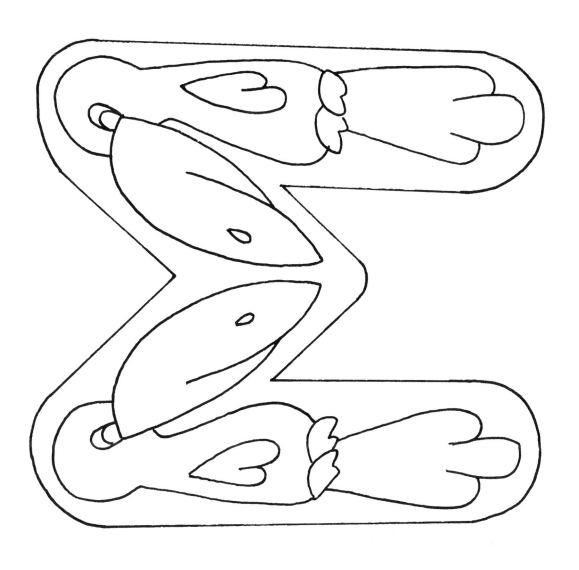

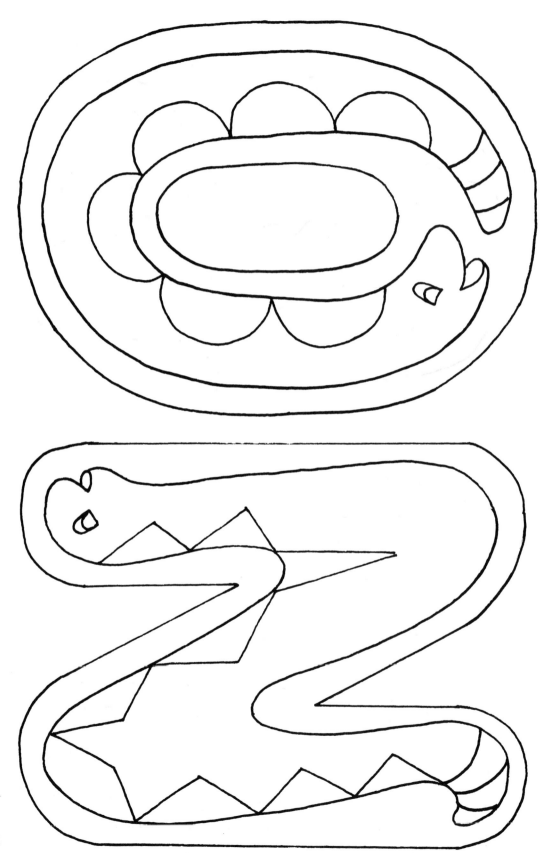

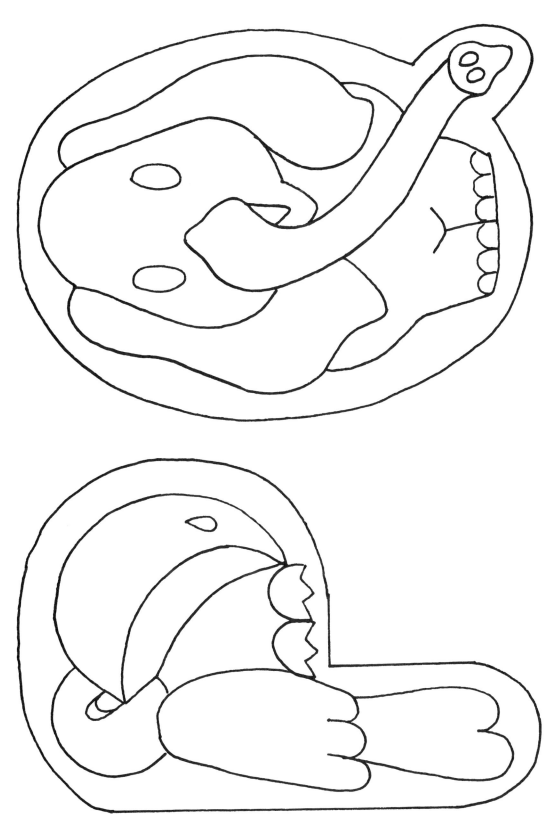

143

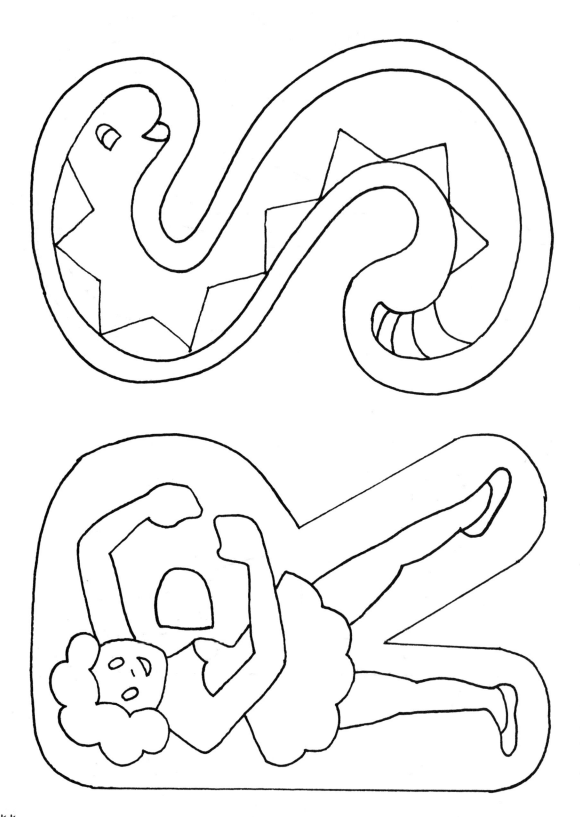

144

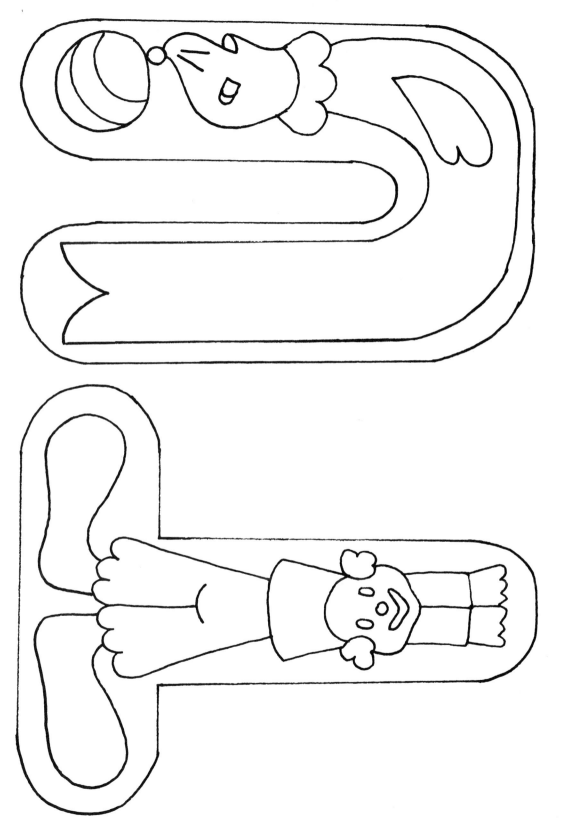

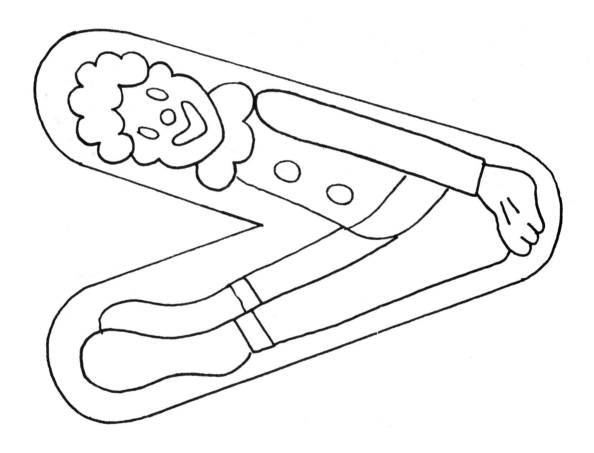

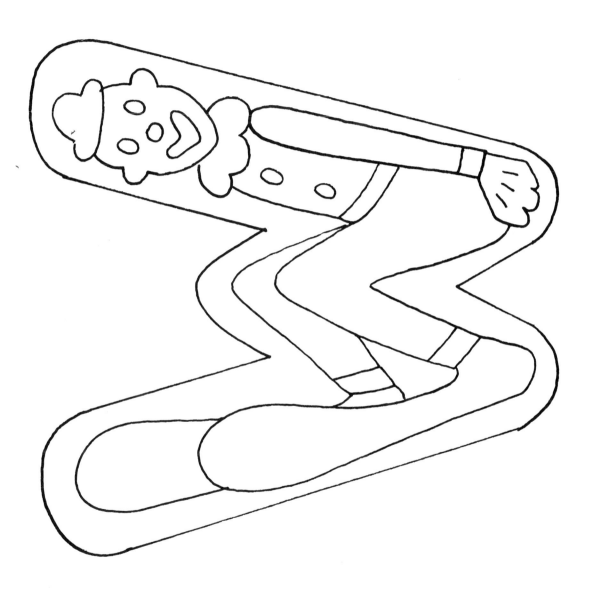

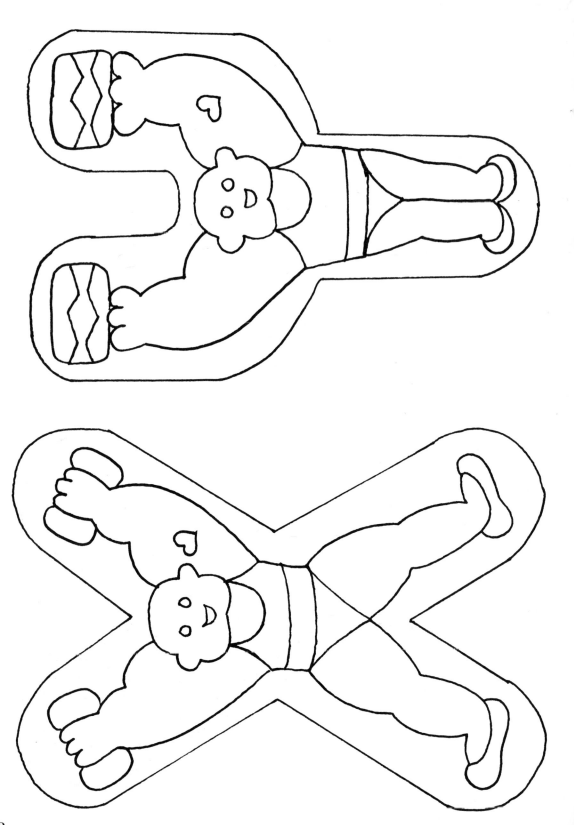

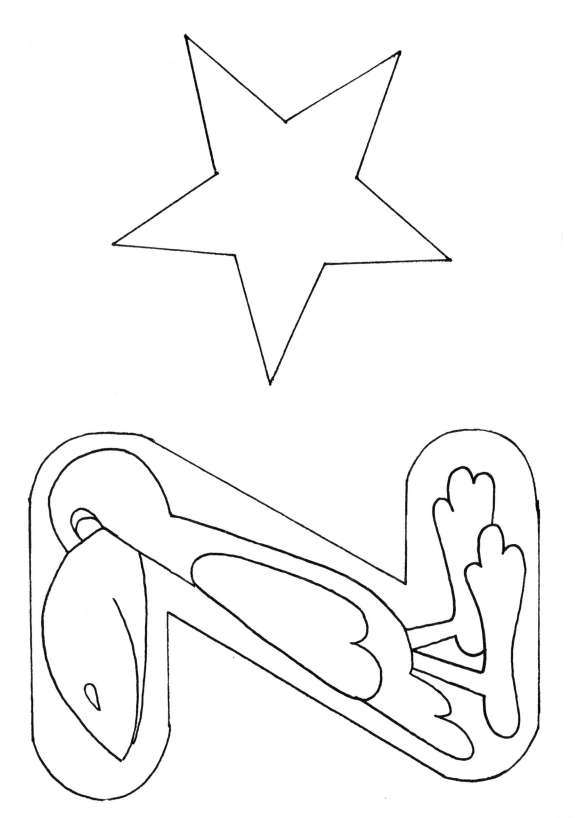

149